Urban
Peak
FDC

THE COMMONS
In Honor
Dick & Karen Thomas and David

ORO Editions
Publishers of Architecture, Art, and Design
Gordon Goff: Publisher

www.oroeditions.com
info@oroeditions.com

Published by ORO Editions

Book Design: **Broz** (**www.brozknows.com**)
Editing: **Chelsey Baker-Hauck**
Art & Graphic Images: **Catalina Lopez**
Architectural Drawings: **Jamie Wallace & Steph Pham**
Photography: **Matthew Staver Photography** (**www.matthewstaver.com**); **all images feature projects designed by Shopworks Architecture**

Featured Projects: **The talented and dedicated team at Shopworks designing for dignity every day**

10 9 8 7 6 5 4 3 2 First Edition

ISBN: **978-1-961856-95-0**

Prepress and Print work by ORO Editions Inc. Printed in China.
ORO Editions Inc. Project Manager: **Jake Anderson**

ORO Editions makes a continuous effort to minimize the overall carbon footprint of its publications. As part of this goal, ORO, in association with Global ReLeaf, arranges to plant trees to replace those used in the manufacturing of the paper produced for its books. Global ReLeaf is an international campaign run by American Forests, one of the world's oldest nonprofit conservation organizations. Global ReLeaf is American Forests' education and action program that helps individuals, organizations, agencies, and corporations improve the local and global environment by planting and caring for trees.

designing for dignity

elements of practice

Daniel Brisson, PhD, MSW | University of Denver
Chad Holtzinger, AIA | Shopworks Architecture
Rachelle Macur, MCA | Shopworks Architecture
Tom Otteson, AIA| Shopworks Architecture
Laura Rossbert, MDiv | Shopworks Architecture
Rachel Speer, PhD, LCSW, MSW | Bryn Mawr College
Stacey Twigg, NCIDQ | Shopworks Architecture
Jennifer Wilson, PhD, MSW | Shopworks Architecture

ORO
EDITIONS

table of **contents**

prologue & introduction ... **1**

sensory engagement ... **8**

1. clear **sightlines** ... **10**
2. enriched **lighting** ... **18**
3. intentional **colors** ... **24**
4. living **systems** ... **30**
5. natural **materials** ... **36**
6. natural **ventilation** ... **42**
7. noise **modulation** ... **46**

nested layers ... **54**

8. accessible **front desk** ... **56**
9. active **security measures** ... **60**
10. approachable **entryway** ... **66**
11. attention to **neglected spaces** ... **72**
12. dedicated **staff places** ... **80**
13. diverse **common areas** ... **86**
14. hearth-like **places** ... **92**
15. multiple **pathways** ... **100**
16. thoughtful **proportions** ... **106**
17. varied **outdoor environments** ... **114**

identity anchors ... **122**

18. charismatic **places** ... **124**
19. clear **wayfinding** ... **130**
20. furnished **apartments** ... **136**
21. personalized **entrances** ... **140**
22. resonant **art** ... **144**

annotated **plans** ... **152**

conclusion ... **166**

appendix ... **168**

acknowledgments

Thank you to our many community and industry partners, including the generous residents, participants, and staff in housing and shelter settings who continue to share their experiences and expertise with our team. We are also so grateful to the nonprofits, developers, and others we work with who allow us to research each of our projects toward a greater understanding of Dignified Design.

We are deeply thankful for our visionary funders who make this research possible: Kaiser Permanente, the Colorado Housing and Finance Authority, and a special thanks to the Sozosei Foundation whose leadership in decriminalizing homelessness has provided inspiration and direction to our team and many others and whose support directly catalyzed this publication.

Finally, we extend our most sincere gratitude to the thought leaders whose contributions have advanced the field and directly impacted our work, including Dr Sam Grabowska, Manifolding Labs; Dr Jill Pable and Dr Yelena McLane, Design Resources for Homelessness; Dr Christina Bollo, University of Oregon; Tye Farrow, Farrow Partners Architects; and Preservation of Affordable Housing.

prologue

Shopworks Architecture was founded in Denver, Colorado, in 2012, with the sole intention of creating life-affirming spaces through life-affirming processes. Today, Shopworks' portfolio is largely comprised of affordable and supportive housing developments along with shelters and social service settings. Our firm continues to partner with community members across the country in the cocreation of environments that seek to honor the dignity and daily realities of human life. A critical and evolving component of our design process has centered on the exploration of trauma-informed and dignified design practices. In-house, and with partners from other firms and institutions, we began studying these practices, seeking input from individuals with lived experience to directly inform how the built environment can serve and sustain or hinder and harm occupants. We continue to test and iterate on these ideas as a team and, importantly, as part of a global community of research and practice. This book reflects our current and best thoughts on and applications of Dignified Design. It represents a point-in-time contribution to a much larger discussion about the role of the built environment as a first responder in somatic regulation and the responsibility of architecture and design to bias people and communities over code and expediency.

introduction

defining **dignity**

Dignity is a state of being, a quality of humanness inherent to each individual. It describes a sense of value, worth, honor, and respect for one's personhood—how we all individually navigate, independently experience, and uniquely perceive the world around us. In this sense, dignity cannot be given or extended, taken or lost. Rather, it is the ultimate quality of being, a celebration of the human spirit, and the potential of each of us to live as fully as we define and determine.

Dignity in design, therefore, requires an intentional examination of the human experience—how we process information and connect with the world around us, how we fundamentally seek survival and pleasure in all we do, how we react in the presence of adversity and stress, surprise and delight. And with this understanding comes empathy for what it means to navigate the world as a complex, conscious, affectable human being. What, then, is our responsibility in designing environments for complex, affectable humans?

2

what is **dignified design**

Dignified Design recognizes the role of our built environment in supporting and fostering health—the health of individuals, neighborhoods and communities, and, ideally, all living things. It acknowledges that nothing we design is neutral and that the places we inhabit shape our ideas about who we are and what we deserve. As an ideal, **Dignified Design aims to create places that protect, promote, and celebrate the dignity of life**.

Dignified Design draws on the broad multidisciplinary evidence of neuroscience and psychology, anthropology and ecology, and of course architecture and design as well as on the more context-specific lived expertise of end users in the spaces we design to deeply understand the entangled relationships between brain, body, culture, and environment. At its core, Dignified Design prioritizes physical and psychological safety and security through the experiences of comfort, community, and control for the people experiencing the building. What, then, are the design tools for tangibly rendering comfort, community, and control? We believe that these core principles can be physically manifested via discrete design features categorized as sensory engagement, nested layers, and identity anchors (which serve as the section headings of this book). These categories are further expressed via 22 distinct design elements that, when employed with intention and balance, create generous environments fostering connection and inviting choice.

an intentional shift toward **dignified design**

Our team has long framed our research as *trauma-informed design*:

1) as a direct companion to and result of the evidence-based practice of "trauma-informed care" often implemented in the programs and services delivered by our clients.
2) acknowledging that a trauma-informed lens is essential for serving the clients of our clients (who are navigating shelters, supportive and affordable housing, and other supportive services).
3) in recognition of the design community's shared understanding and embrace of this term.

All of this still holds true in our work. The need to deeply understand the role of chronic, toxic, and traumatic stress and its effects on our physical and mental wellbeing remains essential—and the role of design in minimizing triggers, communicating "safety," and supporting somatic regulation is critical.

However, it is time to reframe the narrative to center on health and wholeness, to focus on flourishing and thriving, and to prioritize and stipulate a standard of DIGNITY in all environments. As such, Dignified Design is not reserved for "them over there"—**it's about health and hope for *all of us***.

an overview of **this book**

In 2022, our research team initiated a comprehensive study, funded by the Sozosei Foundation, to identify specific features of Dignified Design in housing.

Five supportive housing developments across Colorado were selected to represent a range of trauma-informed and non-trauma-informed design in urban and suburban settings as well as housing authority and nonprofit-operated programs. Three of the housing developments were created with an intentional, trauma-informed Dignified Design approach, while the other two developments represented a more traditional design approach for supportive housing.

Researchers with Dignified Design expertise collected observational data at each of the five sites to identify specific design elements that communicate the core principles of Dignified Design: safety, comfort, community, and control. The data were then analyzed and organized into the 22 distinct elements of Dignified Design featured in this book.

The 22 Elements of Dignified Design uncovered in this study are organized under the three overarching design categories: Sensory Engagement, Nested Layers, and Identity Anchors. Each section begins with a detailed description of the design category, under which the family of design elements is listed. This organizational approach seeks to provide additional clarity and structure for how, when, where, and why to implement each of the 22 Elements.

There is unmistakable complexity in how the various elements weave through and overlap with one another. They are not intended to operate as stand-alone design features. Rather, our research has found that rich experiences of physical and psychological safety exist in the authentic and complex layering of comfort, community, and control. For example, a lobby may be experienced as safe when coupled with a generous and comfortable mix of sensory inputs, easy access to staff via an inviting connection point, and opportunities to exercise choice when navigating space. Features solely intended to promote security (without attention to comfort, community, or control) can become stark, sterile, and institutional—decidedly insecure and unsafe in their presentation. This concept is further outlined in the case diagrams at the back of this book.

Further, the 22 Elements outlined in this book are not intended to be exhaustive or all-encompassing. Without a doubt, there are additional design elements capable of solving for safety, comfort, community, and control in diverse settings. However, these 22 Elements in particular have been repeatedly observed, both in this study and our broader research, as expressions of dignity in the design of housing, shelters, and other social service spaces.

The research we've conducted over the years continues to reinforce that Dignified Design is not a one-size-fits-all solution. It would be impossible to create a checklist to meet the distinct safety, comfort, community, and control definitions and needs of diverse individuals in unique buildings and communities. Rather, the 22 Elements illustrate a range of potential spatial responses and relationships with infinite applications, all of which underscore that Dignified Design requires intention, iteration, and evaluation to achieve meaningful impact.

ARROYO VILLAGE

The **22 Elements** have been organized under the three organizing **principles of Dignified Design,** which are described at the start of each new section:

sensory engagement

1. clear **sightlines**
2. enriched **lighting**
3. intentional **colors**
4. living **systems**
5. natural **materials**
6. natural **ventilation**
7. noise **modulation**

nested layers

8. accessible **front desk**
9. active **security measures**
10. approachable **entryway**
11. attention to **neglected spaces**
12. dedicated **staff places**
13. diverse **common areas**
14. hearth-like **places**
15. multiple **pathways**
16. thoughtful **proportions**
17. varied **outdoor environments**

identity anchors

18. charismatic **places**
19. clear **wayfinding**
20. furnished **apartments**
21. personalized **entrances**
22. resonant **art**

A quick note about **Universal Design**—Universal Design, while too broad to be considered a stand-alone element of Dignified Design, is essential in the creation of spaces that are safe, comfortable, accessible, and dignified. A vital competency for the design of all housing, Universal Design (also referred to as Inclusive Design) embraces a cross-disability approach that supports a diversity of disabilities and celebrates personal choice about what best meets individual needs. While Dignified Design shares many of the values and practices of Universal Design, we recognize that a Dignified Design approach is strengthened by deeper attention to the established principles of this partner process.

sensory engagement

1. clear **sightlines**
2. enriched **lighting**
3. intentional **colors**
4. living **systems**
5. natural **materials**
6. natural **ventilation**
7. noise **modulation**

The experience of trauma is often accompanied by sensory sensitivity and feelings of overstimulation. For some, intense sensory inputs can feel like a threat to their safety or an assault on their peace of mind. When this happens, people can more easily enter a fight, flight, or freeze stress response. Their nervous system may become hypersensitive, responding with contracted muscles; shallow, rapid breathing; dissociation from the environment, and shutting down.

In these cases, our aim is to positively engage the senses—sight, sound, smell, taste, touch, and movement—through gentle stimulation while avoiding overstimulation. Research shows that enriched, sensory engaging environments increase neural connections, enhance neural plasticity, stimulate the production of "happy" brain chemicals, improve learning and cognitive functioning, and improve regulation of our stress responses.

The goal is not to remove all stimuli, creating unnatural, inhospitable, institutional environments. We also want to avoid overstimulation of certain sensory inputs and under stimulation of other inputs. Often, people are overstimulated visually and auditorily, while the rest of their senses are under engaged, causing disorientation and mental fatigue.

Ideally, design elements can be used to offer people a subtle yet engaging sensory journey through a space.

clear **sightlines**

Providing **clear sightlines and prospect** (that is, unimpeded views over a distance for surveillance and planning) allows individuals to assess **both opportunities and challenges** and make choices based on that information. This helps people to anticipate and gain control over their next steps, promoting a sense of safety and agency. Designing for clear sightlines is **one of the most critical** of the elements, given its direct role in promoting all of the primary Dignified Design outcomes (safety, comfort, community, and control).

considerations

Consider the experience of approaching the building's entrance. Ensure that ample attention is given to the physical and mental transition of entering a place, promoting transparency and reducing "leaps of faith."

Use deliberate lighting and large windows to provide visual access into and out of the building so people can see who and what they're about to encounter (sightlines into) as well as who and what is approaching (sightlines out of). Once inside the building, consider sightlines across the multiple pathways that occupants can take to navigate and exit the space.

Map sightlines from key staff areas to the various amenities and gathering spaces to ensure there are eyes on regularly occupied community spaces to promote safety and accountability.

Create opportunities for prospect from nooks, booths, and other places of refuge along the edges of common areas, allowing residents to absorb and participate in the central activities as desired.

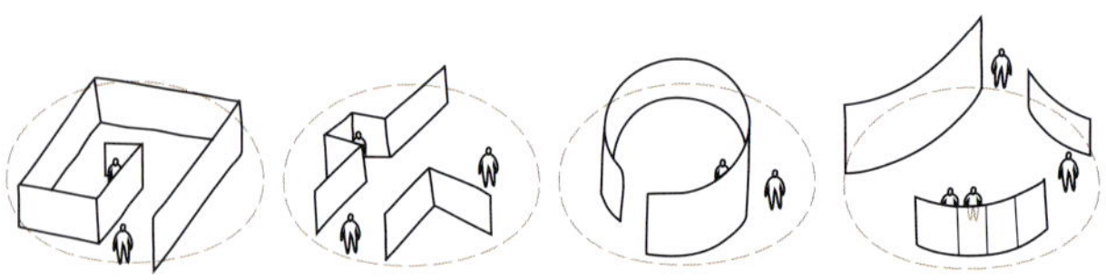

1

1

1

enriched **lighting**

Providing **well-distributed, consistent, and thoughtfully designed lighting** enhances both real and perceived safety and is an opportunity to bring comfort, beauty, control, and charm to a place.

considerations

Consider the color, flexibility, quality, distribution (direct or diffuse), and playfulness of the lighting to provide a sense of place that supports the tasks at hand, such as relaxation, focus, or wayfinding.

Avoid overuse of cool-temperature lighting and recessed fluorescent light fixtures, which can feel institutional and unwelcoming.

Give residents access to abundant daylight to help connect their circadian rhythms to natural daylight cycles, improving cognitive functioning, mood, sleep, and mental fatigue. Daylight should be carefully organized, providing a sparkle without being blindingly bright or overly hot.

Provide choice and control over lighting and daylighting, giving residents the ability to modulate light levels with dimmer switches in community rooms and apartments as well as blackout shades in bedrooms. This is critical for individuals who are sensitive to light due to ocular conditions or migraine headaches.

Be sure that spaces without multiple entry and exit points have adequate lighting and that areas commonly known to feel unsafe for residents, such as parking lots, smoking areas, stairwells, corridors, laundry and trash rooms, are properly illuminated.

Ensure there is sufficient lighting around the building so residents and guests have visual command of their environment as they approach the entrance and move around the property. Provide a well-lit entryway to support safety and wayfinding while also offering incoming residents and guests a view of the activities happening both inside and outside the building.

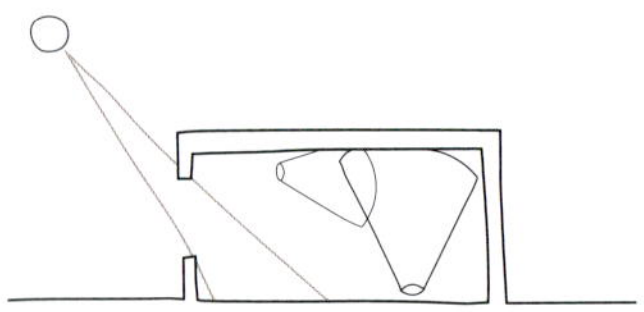

2

2

intentional **colors**

No colors are off limits—no color is inherently trauma-informed. The goal of designing with color is to be **intentional and responsive** to the intended experience, the use of the space, and the needs of those using it.

considerations

Add color in the form of paint, art, lighting, and materials, which can serve as points of delight that spark joy and enhance the personality of a place.

Use color to cultivate a particular emotional experience, invoking a connection to nature, a calming/pacifying experience, or a playful/exciting environment.

Consider residents' histories, cultural identities, and other contextual factors that may inform existing connections to color, including negative connotations associated with particular colors.

Be mindful of potential sensitivities to intense sensory inputs, like bright colors or bold patterns, which may be associated with neurodivergence or brain injury.

LIGHT
BRICK
VENEER
P
LIFE
HUNDERTWASSER.
P

3

3

living **systems**

There are countless benefits to surrounding ourselves with living systems. This connection to life and other living beings is **essential to our health and can be central to the healing process**. When residents can connect with and care for other living systems, such as pets and plants, it can foster a sense of ownership, purpose, and pride through a nurturing cycle of generosity and reciprocity.

considerations

Provide access to plants both inside and outside the building, enhancing the environment's visual complexity, sound attention, and air quality while filling it with natural fractals (repeated geometric patterns found in the world around us at varying scales).

In outdoor spaces, consider installing a community garden or lush, sensory-engaging vegetation. Trees also provide much-needed shade, allowing residents to spend more time outside.

Indoors, fill common areas and corridors with easy-to-maintain plants.

Provide access to other living systems through indigenous plants, wildlife-friendly corridors, bird feeders, pollinator gardens, fish tanks, and/or on-site therapy animals. These can invite and restore broken connections to wildlife and local ecosystems.

Support residents' needs and desires to care for pets through building policies and amenities. Human-animal bonds are shown to promote immense social, physical, and mental health benefits. Whether or not pets are explicitly allowed in leases, many residents will have pets for service, emotional support, or therapy. Create spaces that allow residents to be good pet owners by accounting for noise, waste, and physical activity, providing clear signage and safe walking paths. Shared spaces, like dog runs, allow pets to facilitate connections between neighbors.

Ensure that the care of living systems is properly budgeted (in terms of time and funds) so they don't become a trigger in their neglect or decay.

4

EXIT

4

4

natural materials

Being in nature and around natural materials, such as **wood, stone, plants, and water,** provides a sensory-enriching environment that reduces stress, calms and focuses the mind, and brings us back into our bodies, allowing us to be more **grounded in the environment and present in the here and now**. When in fractal fluency (a level of visual complexity found in biomorphic patterns that humans are biologically drawn to), physiological stress levels are substantially reduced, fostering a state of "wakeful relaxation."

considerations

Create a porous, multisensory experience through natural materials. The use of natural materials draws people in and encourages them to interact and explore, providing authentic sensory feedback and an experience of grounding.

Incorporate natural materials, fractals, and biomorphic patterns through art, furniture and finishings.

Natural materials can be used as a buffer to minimize and modulate sensory input, such as sounds and smells.

Avoid expansive use of drywall and paint, or painted metals, when creating environments that hope to foster intimacy and connection.

Be creative with furniture and finishes by incorporating wood, fabric, copper, stone, and grass—materials that present complex and evolving sensory feedback in terms of texture, hue, patina, and temperature.

5

BLUEBIRD

5

5

As opposed to static and uniform thermal environments, **dynamic airflow and natural ventilation create an enhanced and healthful sensory experience,** fresh air, efficient temperature control, and a physical connection to place.

considerations

Install operable windows in all apartments for fresh air and thermal control and to help alleviate odors. This is an essential component of Dignified Design, supporting individual comfort and personal agency in one's home.

Think of a natural ventilation system as a circuit needing two separate supply and exhaust openings. Consider the location of the supply and exhaust to maximize stack effect (a passive ventilation technique that uses air pressure differences to move air through a building) and minimize the obstruction of airflow.

Foster an indoor–outdoor connection with garage doors or other large door or window openings from common areas to outdoor amenity spaces that support comfortable all-season interactions with the elements.

Use natural ventilation, to modulate temperatures in places of transition and avoid the unpleasantness of an abrupt change. For example, a vestibule should begin to bridge the thermal experience (e.g., temperature and humidity) from the lobby to the outdoors.

natural ventilation

6

6

Properly accounting for noise is **critical for minimizing overstimulation and negative physiological responses**. Spaces that are loud and reverberate can feel chaotic, overwhelming, and threatening, triggering people's stress response. On the other hand, it's not desirable to completely eliminate noise, which creates an unnatural, sterile environment. The goal is to thoughtfully **filter and modulate acoustic inputs** in ways that promote curiosity and exploration, allowing people to receive acoustical feedback from the task at hand without being assaulted by every adjacent noise.

considerations

Utilize structural soundproofing between walls and floors, absorptive wall treatments (such as acoustic panels or felt wall coverings) and intentional furniture and finish materials (including wood, fabric, and plants) to filter and modulate noise.

Consider the angles of surfaces, which can help with sound attenuation. Layered ceiling heights and nonparallel planes dissipate sound waves, dampening noise and echoes.

Positively incorporate noise into common areas with intentional music or soundscapes. Natural sounds, like bubbling water, birdsong, wind chimes (via open windows), and crackling fires, introduce stress-reducing, life-giving qualities into a space.

noise modulation

7

EXIT

7

EXIT

7

EXIT

7

nested layers

8. accessible **front desk**
9. active **security measures**
10. approachable **entryway**
11. attention to **neglected spaces**
12. dedicated **staff places**
13. diverse **common areas**
14. hearth-like **places**
15. multiple **pathways**
16. thoughtful **proportions**
17. varied **outdoor environments**

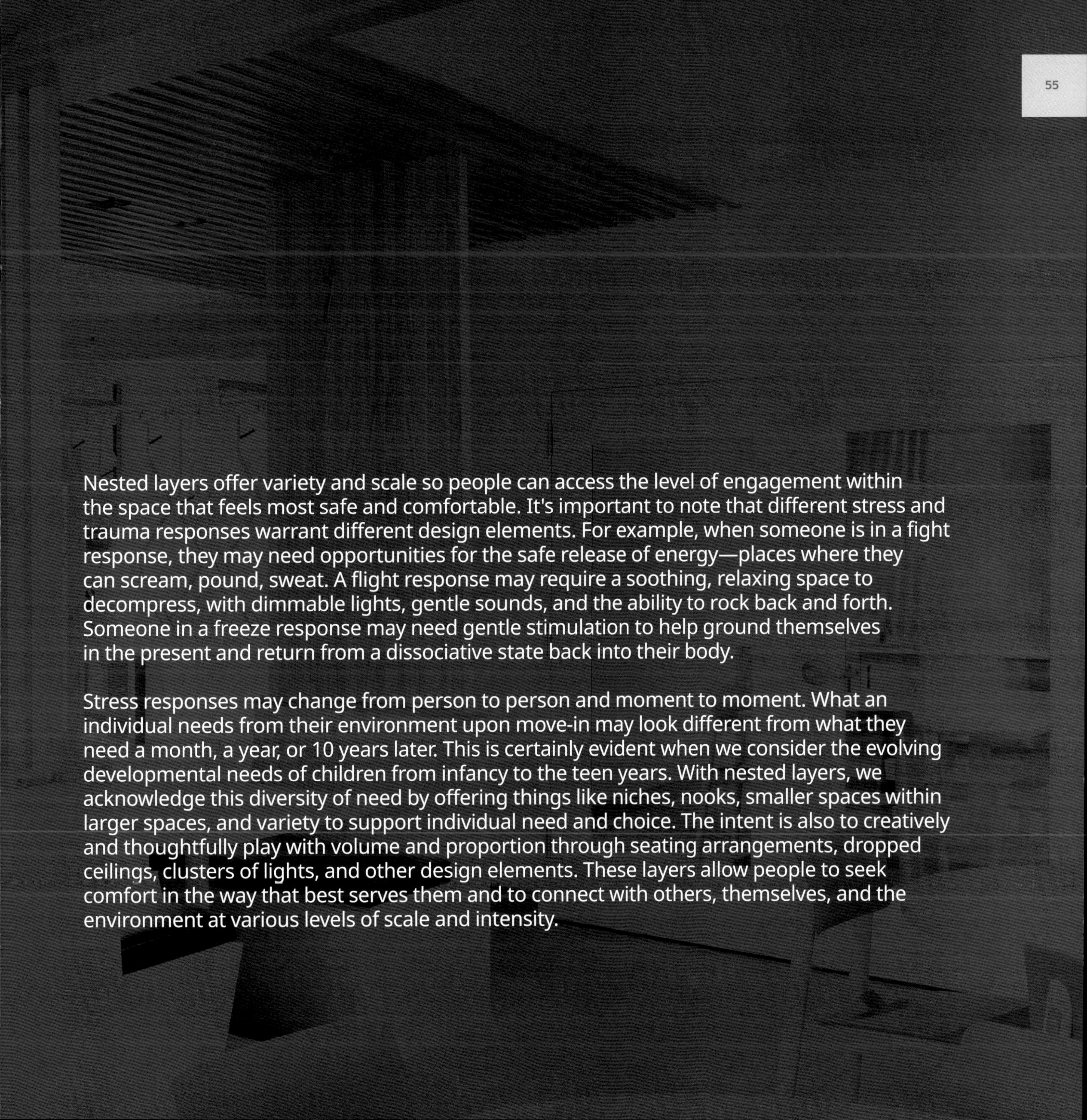

Nested layers offer variety and scale so people can access the level of engagement within the space that feels most safe and comfortable. It's important to note that different stress and trauma responses warrant different design elements. For example, when someone is in a fight response, they may need opportunities for the safe release of energy—places where they can scream, pound, sweat. A flight response may require a soothing, relaxing space to decompress, with dimmable lights, gentle sounds, and the ability to rock back and forth. Someone in a freeze response may need gentle stimulation to help ground themselves in the present and return from a dissociative state back into their body.

Stress responses may change from person to person and moment to moment. What an individual needs from their environment upon move-in may look different from what they need a month, a year, or 10 years later. This is certainly evident when we consider the evolving developmental needs of children from infancy to the teen years. With nested layers, we acknowledge this diversity of need by offering things like niches, nooks, smaller spaces within larger spaces, and variety to support individual need and choice. The intent is also to creatively and thoughtfully play with volume and proportion through seating arrangements, dropped ceilings, clusters of lights, and other design elements. These layers allow people to seek comfort in the way that best serves them and to connect with others, themselves, and the environment at various levels of scale and intensity.

accessible **front desk**

The **design of the front desk is critical to Dignified Design,** particularly in housing, as it's often the first encounter an individual has with the building and staff. Their experience of and relationship with the front desk **can set the tone** for how they feel about and engage with the building and community. In addition, the front desk must balance accessibility and approachability for residents with the safety and job requirements of staff.

considerations

Select a front desk location that offers staff clear visual access to those approaching and entering the front door as well as sightlines across the first floor, prioritizing access to common areas like the lobby, elevators, mailboxes, stairwells, public restrooms, and staff offices. Ideally, the front desk and/or staff areas would also have visual access to shared outdoor spaces, including parking lots and play areas.

Ensure there is enough room for circulation through the front door as well as for multiple co-occurring interactions at the desk. This area is often one of the busiest in a building and needs room to breathe.

Scale the front desk to feel inviting and available to residents on foot and in wheelchairs and to children who may need to connect with a staff member.

Create adjacent meeting space should a sensitive conversation need to be transitioned from the desk to a more private nearby location.

Design desks to provide a physical barrier between staff and escalated guests. This can be done through raised counter heights, dropped ceilings, and a secure path for staff to exit from behind. The layout must offer at least two exit routes as well as direct visual and auditory access to other staff when support is needed.

At the front desk, avoid overt institutional features, such as plexiglass or glass partitions that reach to the ceiling. Rather, play with the volume of the space to allow the front desk to feel protected yet inviting.

8

OFFICE

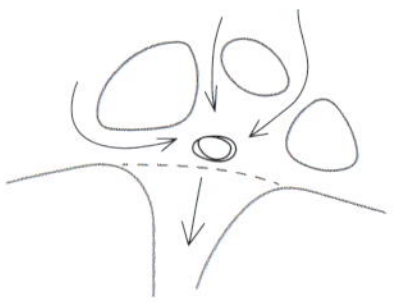

8

active **security measures**

Active security measures are essential to ensuring the safety and security of residents, staff, guests, and visitors. These measures help control access and monitor activities in and around the building. Active security measures should be **paired with more passive safety features that communicate comfort, community, and control**—such as clear sightlines and an accessible front desk. Otherwise, the experience will feel more like forced institutional security rather than the peace of mind associated with home.

considerations

Be thoughtful about access control systems, which are essential for managing traffic through housing. In supportive settings, where staff are actively monitoring a front desk, consider remote access devices that allow staff to move around the building while keeping eyes on the front door.

Plan for security camera coverage in all public areas, including exterior doors, corridors, stairwells, amenity spaces, parking lots, and outdoor areas. Camera coverage is a common request of both residents and staff. Cameras should be visible yet subtle to promote transparency and accountability while avoiding overt suggestions of surveillance.

Adequate indoor and outdoor lighting measures support both real and perceived safety. Motion sensors can create an unpredictable, unsettling experience, so consider controllable, reliable lighting options that residents and staff can manage as needed.

In housing, traditional keys are often preferred for apartment doors, while key fobs or key cards are used for exterior doors and amenities. From a security standpoint, the mechanism for making and copying a traditional key is often known and understood by residents, making them a more familiar, trusted option for apartments. Conversely, key fobs and other technologies are not as well understood and, therefore, can be unsettling for residents.

Consider the proximity of ground-floor apartments to busy roads, sidewalks, and alleyways. Attempt to create buffers and barriers that promote a greater sense of safety and comfort for residents living on the main level. When apartments are situated directly on a busy roadway with heavy foot traffic, consider how the building can be popped up to shield residents physically and visually.

When designing, prepare an adequate budget for cameras, fobs, and automatic hardware. These are essential features that are difficult and invasive to retrofit after a building is complete.

9

RHONDA'S
PLACE
203 S. FEDERAL BLVD.
3000 W
S Federal Blvd
W Cedar Ave
200 S

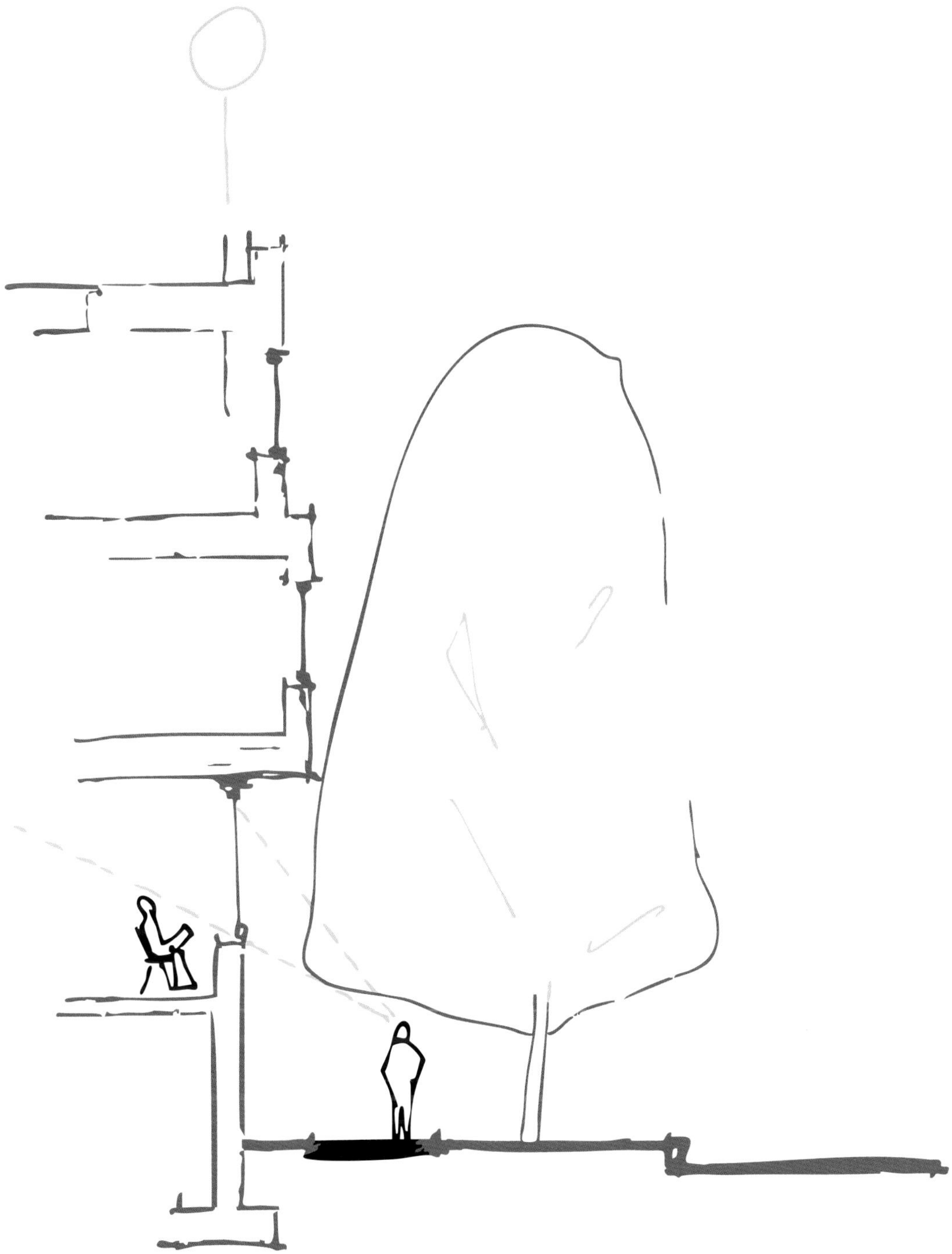

9

approachable **entryway**

Entryways are **archetypal features representing a threshold or gateway** from one environment into another. The character of the entryway sets the tone for the transition and state of arrival. The design of the entryway also **communicates to those entering that they are cared for and their needs matter**.

considerations

Scale entryways to be welcoming, distinct, and approachable, clearly communicating to visitors where they are expected to enter the building without question or mystery.

Offer guests a glimpse of what is coming once they enter the building. Clear visual access from the outside via large windows allows us to begin setting expectations, crafting a plan, and identifying an exit strategy.

Covered entryways generously provide protection from the elements (rain, snow, excessive wind and sun) and communicate a sense of reaching the safe bounds of the threshold.

Provide a bench or seating areas near the entryway where people can wait for rides or visitors, connect with neighbors, or simply participate in the world around them.

Think about safety provisions, such as locked vestibules, intercom systems, access control systems, and visual access to other community members. For some communities, this may mean a secure front desk immediately at the entrance and explicit guest check-in protocols.

Often, the entry is several feet above the sidewalk. Care must be given to ensure the accessible route is equally dignified and not an afterthought.

st valentines
ST VALENTINE APTS
10.17.20

10

THE
FOUNDRY
APARTMENTS
501

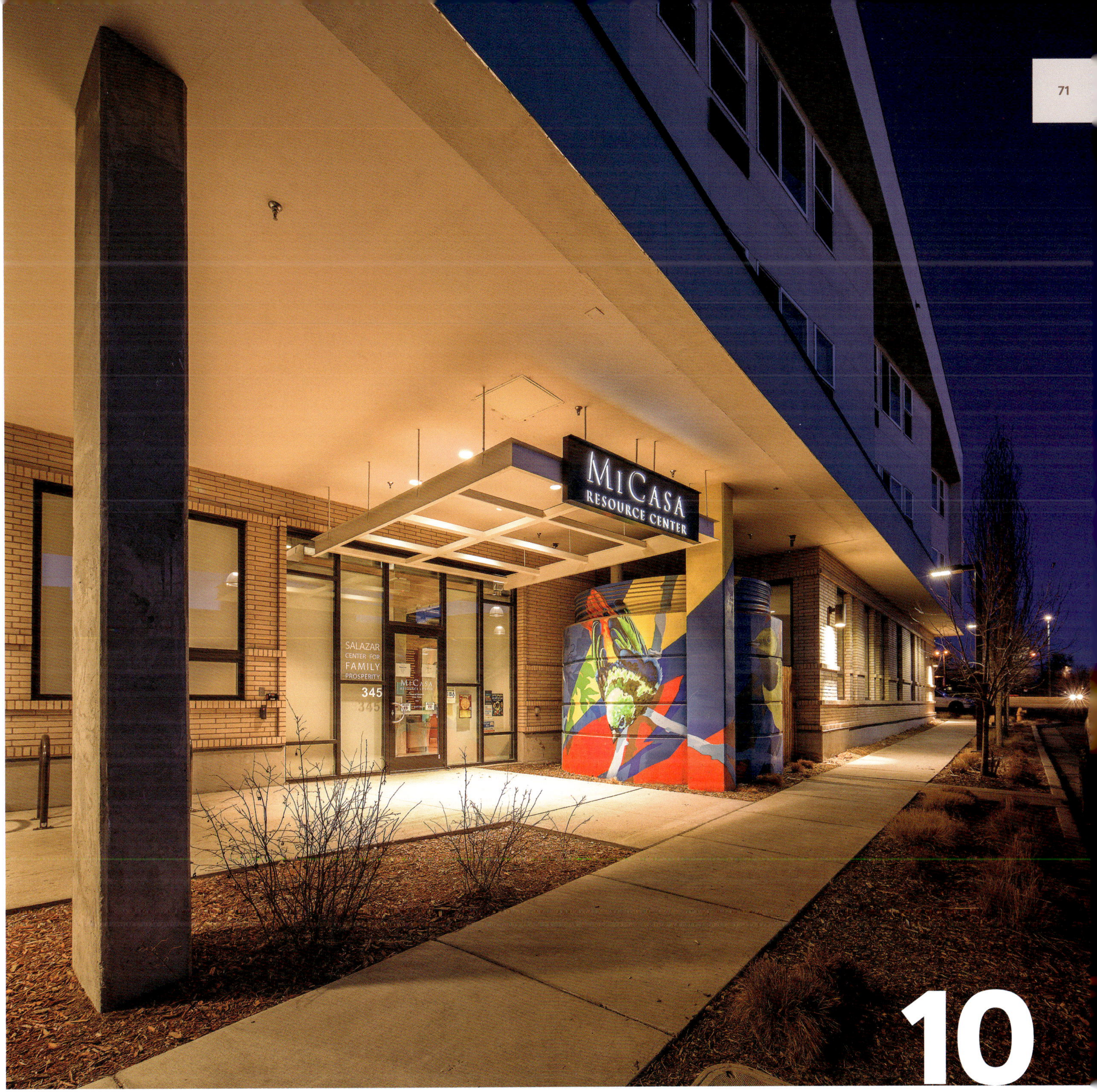
MiCasa
Resource Center
Salazar
Center for
Family
Prosperity
345

10

attention to neglected spaces

Every apartment building has essential spaces—including laundry and trash rooms, mail areas, bike storage, parking, and stairwells—that are used on a regular basis and visited by nearly everyone in the community. Although these spaces define a resident's everyday experience in the building, their design is often overlooked.

considerations

Ensure the design of "neglected spaces" carefully considers security, visual access, accessibility, and opportunities to positively connect with other community members.

View mail areas as opportunities for residents to connect (either directly or indirectly) with other members of the community. These spaces should be situated within direct visual access of staff areas and near a lobby or community room to promote chance encounters with others.

Consider lighting, accessibility, and sightlines in the parking area and the path from a vehicle to the building's entrance with an eye for blind spots and areas difficult to monitor.

Thoughtful placement of dumpsters and trash rooms should support safety and sightlines. Dealing with trash is often described as the most unpleasant (and at times, the least safe) experience residents have in their apartment building. Dare to imagine elements of comfort and delight in these especially neglected spaces.

Create seating and tables in laundry rooms so residents can comfortably wait while their clothes are being cleaned/dried. The space should ideally support the discreet handling of personal items with screens and side areas for folding laundry.

Provide secure storage for bikes, which are often considered a precious asset for maintaining employment, education, social connection, and physical fitness. Many residents will prefer to store them in their apartments or a secure, monitored location. If bike storage is being offered in the building, make it an access-controlled area with sightlines to staff. If bikes can be kept in apartments, install hooks with space to navigate around them.

Create ample, purpose-built storage for both residents and staff to store items such as program materials and donations; resident belongings like off-season clothing, holiday decorations, and kids gear; property management files; and maintenance tools and supplies. Clutter leads to mental fatigue, which is linked to stress, anxiety, and depression, so it is important to support storage options for residents and staff wherever possible.

11

Speed Queen
Commercial Washer
659-JJH
Speed Queen
Commercial Dryer
658-JJH

11

11

U.S. MAIL
APPROVED BY THE POSTMASTER GENERAL

11

dedicated **staff places**

Staff need space to attend to their own needs—to take a break, prepare a meal, make a personal call, decompress, and recoup. For their health and wellbeing, it's essential that staff have privacy from the ongoing demands of service work and are provided with places of restoration. In addition, staff need **flexible meeting places and storage** to be successful at their jobs.

considerations

Incorporate elements of beauty and delight in staff break rooms, which are important for the health and retention of high-quality, committed team members. Resources that support staff care ultimately promote deep empathy and engagement in the work.

Staff often describe a tension between needing real respite from the work while remaining immediately accessible in the event of emergencies. As such, break areas must balance being both removed and connected, situated near common areas with some auditory connection, while distinct and separate.

Provide staff with lockable storage for personal belongings, a full kitchen with a dishwasher and beverage bar (to communicate comfort and care), a private bathroom, and comfortable seating.

Soundproofing is essential in staff areas to ensure auditory privacy for sensitive conversations.

Visual privacy is a more nuanced consideration. Although interior and exterior windows are essential for sightlines and daylighting, strategic window design and coverings are needed for a customizable experience. For some, a small window in the door is preferred; for others, a full window wall may be ideal for inviting residents into the space. This depends on the role of the staff member and the nature of their daily interactions.

Prioritize flexibility in office and meeting spaces. Given the variable nature of the work, staff often prefer a mix of shared open workspace and private offices for more confidential conversations.

Secure, dedicated storage space is often needed for files. Additionally, consider the size and location of storage throughout the building to support programming, access to donated items, and the storage of furniture and furnishings.

12

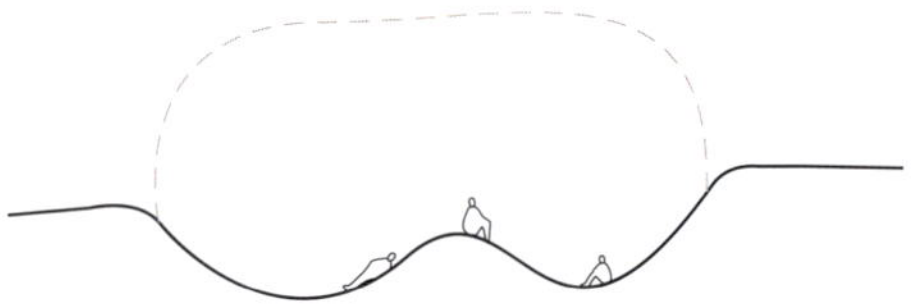

MiCasa
Resource Center
12

indy street flats

12

diverse **common areas**

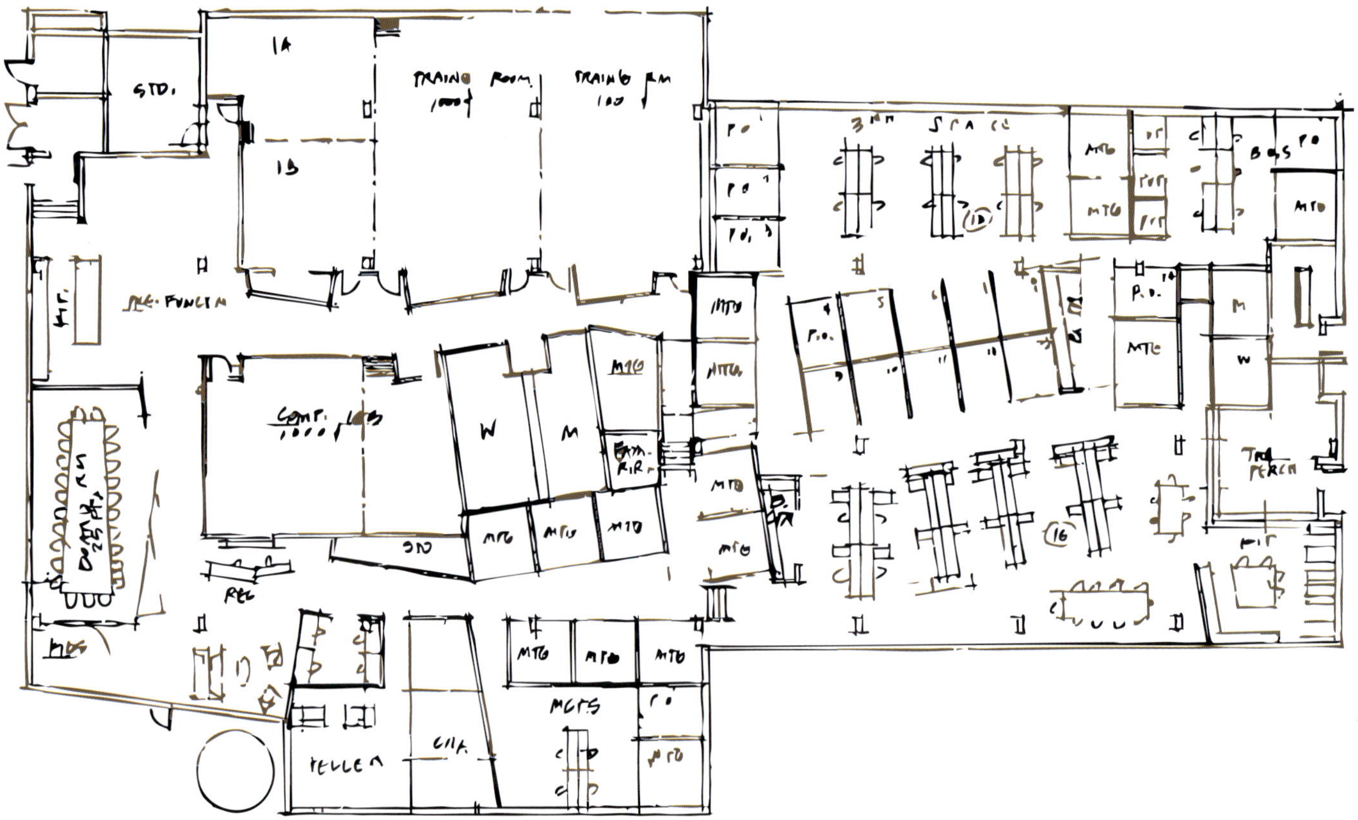

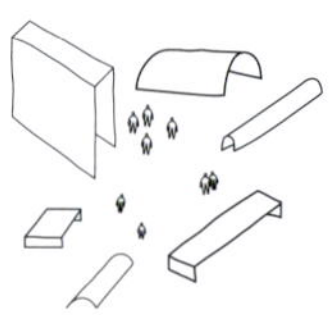

To combat isolation and draw residents out of their apartments, it is critical that **shared spaces promote positive social interactions** between residents, guests, staff, and the surrounding community. For these spaces to be successful, they must be **diverse, connected, flexible, and universal** in their design.

considerations

Consider spaces that will satisfy a range of experiences for all ages and abilities—large and small gatherings, social and solo opportunities, active and serene outlets.

Break up large, open spaces into smaller areas that are more intimate and less intimidating. Dropped ceilings, flooring transitions, clustered seating and lighting help create nested layers where people can find what best meets their presenting needs.

Foster flexibility with easily movable furniture and walls. Anticipate the multiple uses of a space. For example, include a sink in a large room that may be used for art, cooking, or clinics.

Create peripheral seating options and areas of refuge, like booths or small reading nooks, along the edges of larger amenity spaces. This offers places to sidle while still being social, supporting people-watching and semiprivate interactions.

Provide static seating as well as options that support movement. Rhythmic outlets like swings and rocking chairs are known to engage the parasympathetic nervous system and the release of feel-good hormones in the body.

Foster opportunities for casual collision in hallways, stairwells, mail rooms, and other places of transit. Wide hallways and stairwells, seating nooks, art and other materials to engage with, can support organic interactions and the exchange of ideas.

Provide places where service providers can work and meet with residents across the site, both indoors and outdoors. For properties serving families, seating clusters near indoor/outdoor play areas encourage case management and social interactions while children are safely occupied.

Be sure that places for intimate conversations support auditory privacy (via acoustic modulation) as well as a sense of safety and connection outside the room (via interior and exterior windows and controllable window coverings).

13

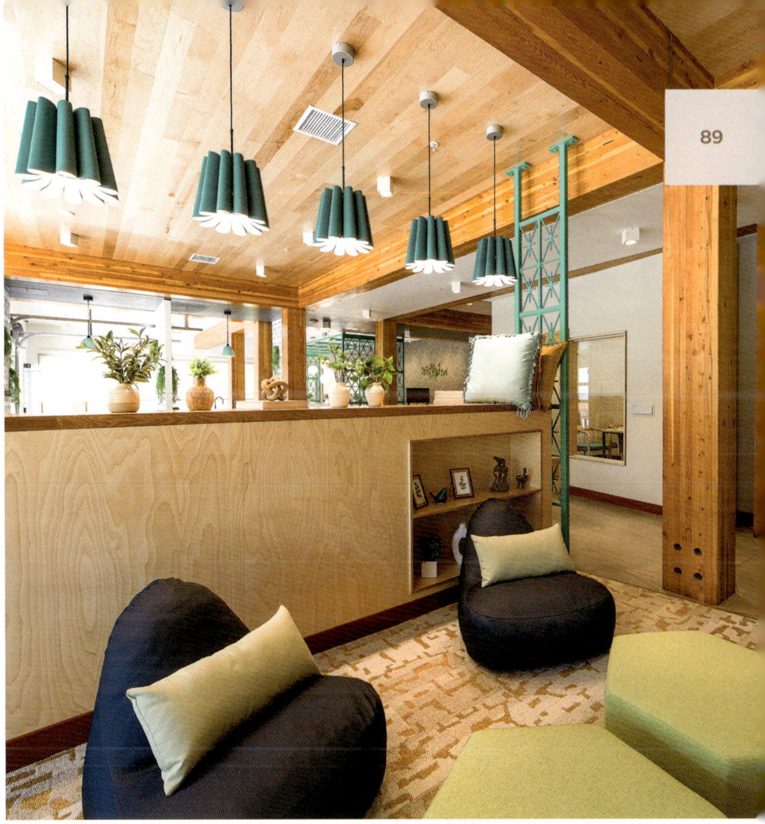

13

Welcome home
WHERE MEMORIES ARE MADE,
TEARS ARE SHED, LOVE IS FELT,
AND REFUGE IS FOUND.
You belong here

13

Hearth-like places embody connection and comfort. Circular seating arrangements provide a **nonhierarchical way to connect** with others, breaking down barriers and encouraging people to share and listen. These spaces invoke feelings of warmth, belonging, and awe, connecting us to our biological roots of storytelling where narratives and myths are created and shared.

considerations

Install fireplaces or outdoor firepits, which provide a nonrhythmic, multisensory experience that relaxes minds and reduces blood pressure.

Provide circular seating arrangements with elements of warmth, such as rocking chairs made of natural materials that foster comfort and respite. Round tables communicate intimacy over a shared meal.

Be creative with circular community spaces, such as rounded community kitchens, bar tops, therapy rooms, or meeting rooms.

Orient these spaces within sightlines of staff areas to promote social accountability and diversity of use. When safe and welcoming, these inherently social features can serve to connect people who may not otherwise associate.

hearth-like **places**

14

14

14

14

For both real and perceived safety, it's important to provide **multiple pathways in and out of regularly used spaces**. This prevents building users from feeling (or being) trapped and offers **choice in how they move through the building** based on their own ability and desire. This promotes safety and reduces conflict.

considerations

Pair this element with clear sightlines and wayfinding so individuals can easily map their exit options. Entries/exits should also have larger transitional spaces, wider doors, and circulation that is free of obstacles.

Provide multiple ways to enter and exit daily-use amenity spaces, such as corridors, laundry rooms, mail areas, and trash rooms where people often feel trapped.

Ensure that all pathways are safe, well lit, accessible, and explicitly inviting. This is especially important for stairwells, which are often viewed as "sewers for egress" but can, instead, be seen as an opportunity to use the building in a healthy and active way.

Provide multiple doorways and exits for staff to quickly leave the front desk, meeting rooms, and their offices if threatened.

multiple **pathways**

15

OFFICE

15

THRIVE
EXIT
START
Jonathan Applegate

15

thoughtful proportions

There is an art to designing spaces that **balance expansiveness and intimacy**. Spaces that are too open can incite feelings of agoraphobia, while spaces that are too closed can feel claustrophobic. Thoughtful proportions demand **responsiveness to both human scale and the context at hand**.

considerations

Scale and proportion must work in service to the principles of safety and comfort, communicating accessibility and approachability over grandeur and ostentation.

Building and spaces should relate to the scale of the human body. Buildings that are too "grand" feel impersonal and promote feelings of isolation, whereas the intimate scale is comfortable and promotes connection.

In large, open spaces, introduce elements of intimacy, such as dropped ceilings, layered light fixtures, sidling spaces, and nooks.

In spaces that are more compressed, provide elements of openness, such as lighter color palettes, expansive patterns, daylight, and view to the outdoors and in the building.

Thinking horizontally, consider balance in the square footage being dedicated to active and interactive places as well as to more intimate, pensive spaces.

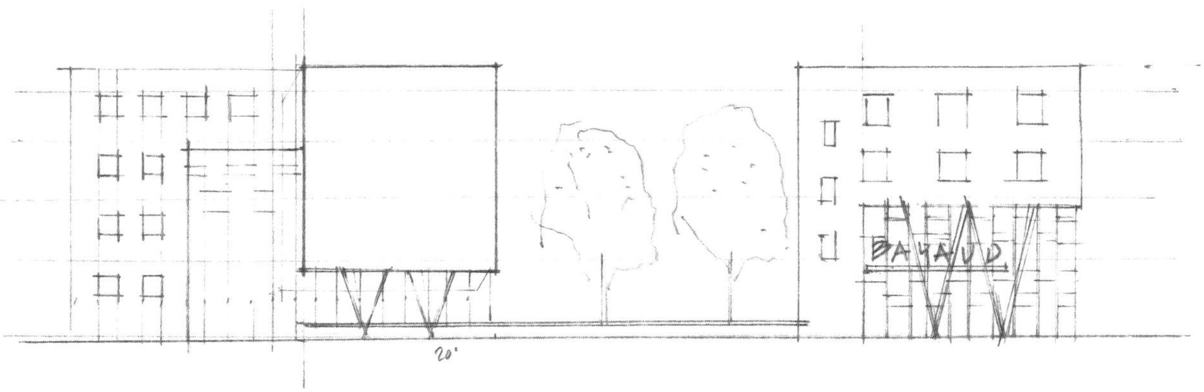

16

LAUREL HOUSE

16

FDC

16

318

16

varied **outdoor environments**

Well-designed outdoor spaces offer a **variety of distinct, usable places** for connecting and socializing, contemplation and respite, movement and play, exploration and discovery. Outdoor spaces should foster a **rich sensory experience,** consider the specific uses and needs of building occupants, and support all life.

considerations

Offer a variety of enriching sensory experiences—places in the shade and places to soak in the sun, places to grill and share a meal and places off to the side to journal quietly, places to climb, and places to gently swing or rock. The creation of outdoor environments is a matter of variety and choice.

Foster biodiversity and a connection to nature through wildlife-friendly elements, such as community gardens, pollinator plantings, birdbaths, native vegetation, restorative rain gardens, bug hotels, or brush that provides homes for burrowing animals. Food forests feature edible plants that children and animals can safely explore.

Consider the diversity of ages and development levels using the space. If the building is serving families, do not forget about welcoming environments for older children and teenagers. Play spaces must be secure and provide visual access for caregivers and staff both inside and outside the building.

Address diverse accessibility needs by offering choice in terms of pathways, seating, and shade. Consider how people in wheelchairs, those who use walkers, and individuals with unsteady gaits might cross different surfaces.

Provide amenities that support positive pet ownership along with the necessary infrastructure, such as trash bins, pet waste bags, and courtesy signage. Safe nighttime access should be supported via proximity to a main entrance, ample lighting, and security fencing. Dog parks/dog runs can strengthen resident ties to their pets as well as to other residents, staff, and animals in the building.

Clearly designated smoking areas support people who smoke as well as those who wish to distance themselves from the activity. Smoking is a known coping strategy for anxiety, depression, chronic pain, and recovery from substances. Dedicated smoking areas are a critical consideration for all supportive housing and shelter settings.

17

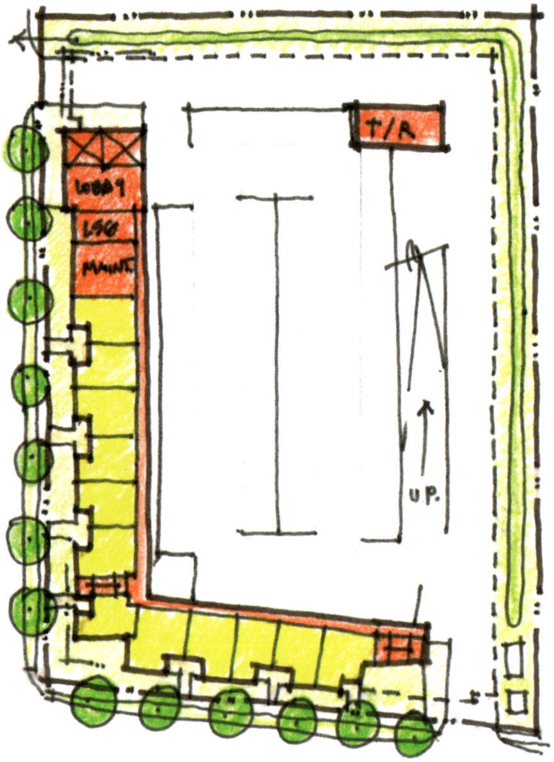

L.1 & 2

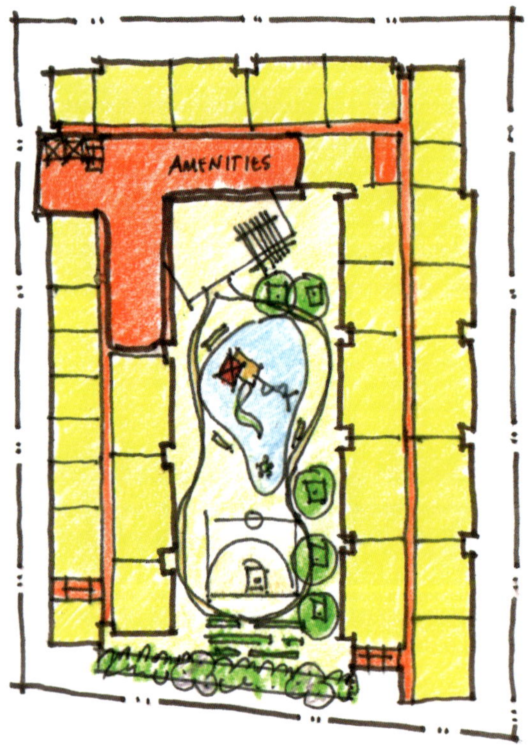

L3-5

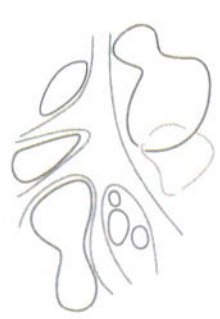

17

EMPOWER
FIELD

17

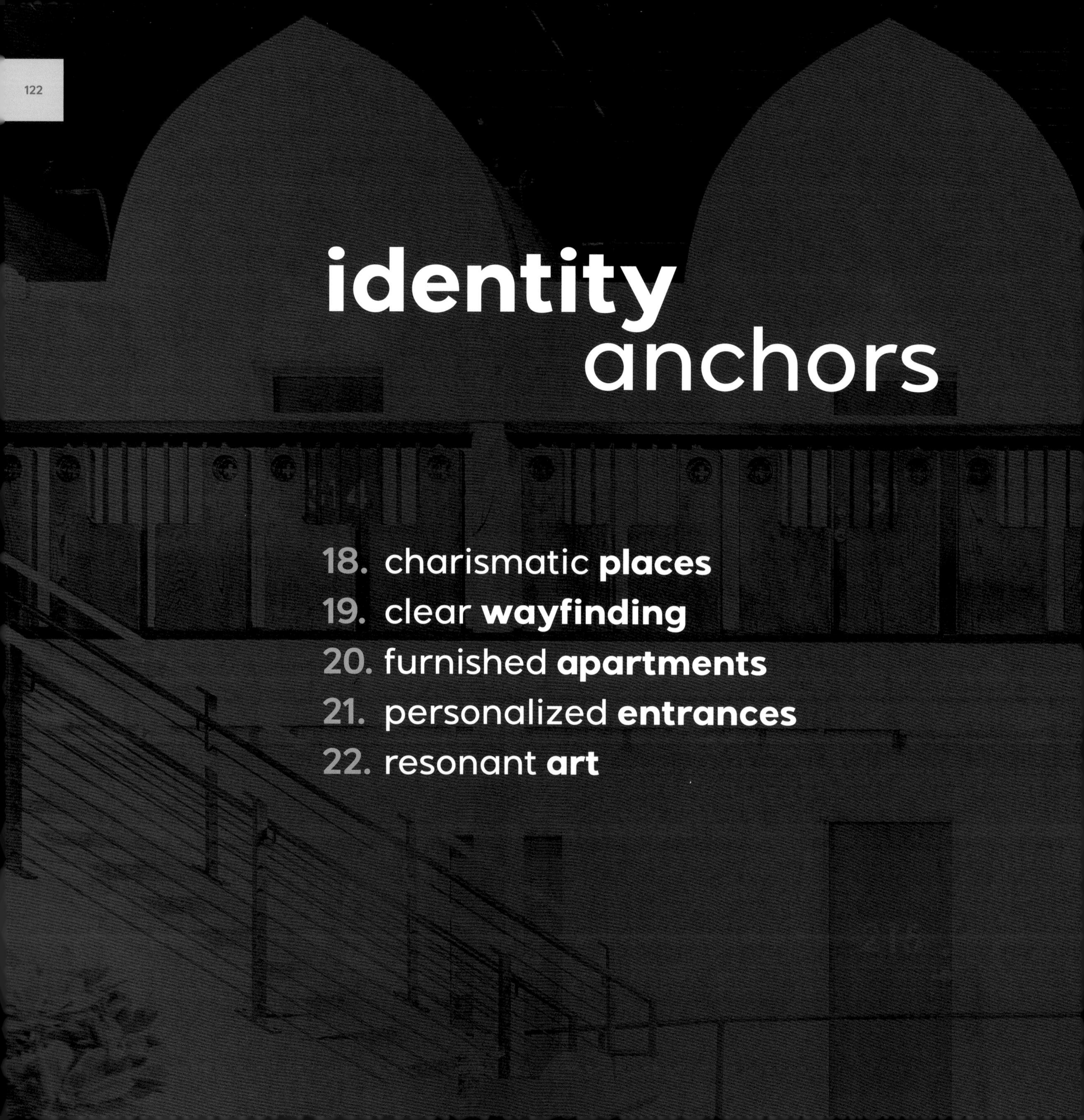

identity anchors

18. charismatic **places**
19. clear **wayfinding**
20. furnished **apartments**
21. personalized **entrances**
22. resonant **art**

Identity anchors are elements that invite residents, staff, visitors, and the surrounding neighborhood to see themselves in the design. They foster a sense of belonging, cultivate an attachment to place and self, and combat isolation—all essential to promoting self-worth, dignity, and healing.

A key aspect of the identity anchor concept is to challenge the design of impersonal, neutral, and generic elements in favor of features that intentionally seek to personalize, reflect, and represent some meaningful aspect of the local context (that is, the people, cultures, and traditions that were and are). The idea is not to reduce identity to a single catch-all feature but to create a constellation of touchpoints where people can see themselves represented throughout the environment.

We must also think about spaces for ritual, reverence, and routine that (re)connect people to themselves and others. This is essential when individuals are moving into a new place and potentially reconstructing their lives, as is so often the case in supportive housing. During these transitions, the relationships that people forge with their homes can be central to their sense of identity, self-worth, and dignity.

This element actively resists a tendency toward neutral design that can feel impersonal, lifeless, and institutional. Instead, it **infuses the environment with life, energy, and a distinct human impression**. Designs bearing a defined and relatable character invite people to forge a conversation and cultivate personal relationships with place. Further, the sterility of perfection, so often communicated in stark design, can suggest that the space is not tolerant of humans and their messiness. **Anomalies and quirks** suggest that the design is for everyone, **celebrating wonder, curiosity, delight, nostalgia, and life**.

considerations

Play with color, texture, strong motifs, and bold styles. This may include vibrant wallpaper designs, distinct furniture styles, playful angles and curves in walls and windows. As always, balance must be a consideration; bold, playful elements used in excess may feel disorienting.

Intentionally introduce sensory and biophilic elements, such as wood beams, playful shadows, textured materials, pleasant sounds and smells, and features that invoke mystery, delight, and awe.

Use authentic materials and indigenous crafts to articulate connection to place. Avoid mass-produced and institutional palettes which tend to be sterile and homogeneous.

Create and maintain themes throughout the building through wayfinding elements, such as signage, room names, and distinct markers for each floor or wing of the building.

Layer elements of identity throughout the building. This can be in the form of imagery, symbols, artifacts, or stories that represent the cultures, values, and histories of the residents and neighborhood. Be mindful to select for authentic connection and avoid imposing the personal bias of the designer.

charismatic **places**

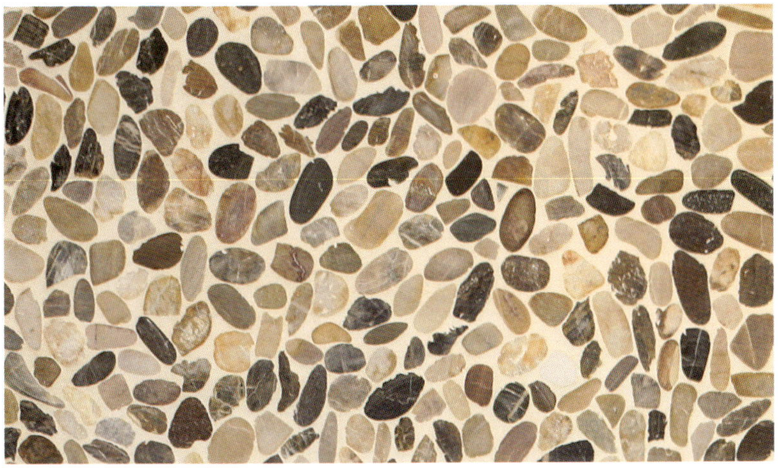

18

Brunch!

18

mail

18

Design elements that support navigation through spaces are **essential to mitigate disorientation and foster a sense of safety and trust**. Knowing where you are and where you're going promotes feelings of groundedness and confidence. Wayfinding can also provide **a gentle transition** while journeying through distinct places and across various thresholds.

considerations

Wayfinding should be intuitive and offer transparency via generous sightlines across indoor and outdoor spaces. It should provide clear indication of how to use the building without the need for signage (yet signage should still be provided).

Offer clear indicators of one's current location and where to go. Indicators can be explicit (such as large signage at the entrance with the building name and address) or more subtle connections to place through symbols and patterns (such as floor numbers posted at all elevator bays and stairwells, clear and easy-to-read apartment numbers, and different colors or themes indicated in the finishes on each floor).

Consider languages and literacy, neurodivergence, and the varied abilities and experiences of all potential residents, guests, and staff. Incorporate braille on signage, visual doorbells for those with hearing impairment, pictograms to support all languages and literacy levels, and signage in multiple languages as needed.

clear **wayfinding**

19

19

EXIT

19

Residents often enter supportive housing with few belongings, if any. **Entering a new home that is empty, and without items of your own to fill it with, can be demoralizing and isolating**. When designing supportive housing in particular, it is strongly recommended that some basic items are provided so residents can take the next steps in their lives knowing that their **essential needs are met**.

considerations

Furnish apartments with a few large furniture items (such as a bed, couch, table and chairs) as well as items that are immediately needed upon move-in (such as linens, towels, and dishes). Comfort items are also strongly recommended, such as a plant or homemade blanket—a human touch in welcoming people to their new home.

Consider body-size diversity when selecting furniture. Twin beds and armchairs may not work for some bodies.

Consider space for medical equipment and other devices supporting health and wellness, including wheelchairs, walkers, oxygen tanks, and CPAP machines (for sleep-related breathing disorders).

Give residents the opportunity to curate their own interior décor. For example, by choosing between two living room furniture sets or selecting their own linens and towels from a collection of new items. If decorative items are donated, such as artwork, include them in a selection of optional furnishings from which residents can "shop." This instills a sense of choice and personalization in the home.

furnished **apartments**

20

20

Individual entrances are a **sacred threshold between the public realm and the private home** and should, therefore, be treated with care and honor. Opportunities for personalized entrances can shift the feeling of an apartment entry from that of an impersonal unit to **a place residents can call "home."** Personalized entrances can communicate the cozy scale of a customized home within a larger, more anonymous building.

considerations

Design entrances to have a distinctive "front porch" through set-back or protruding doors, decorative trim to create a pitched roof or welcoming arch, distinctive colors, and/or a "porchlight."

Varied flooring in front of the door simulates a literal front porch. Functionally, it offers tactile feedback underfoot for those approaching the unit as well as auditory cues for those inside that a visitor is nearing the threshold of their home.

Be mindful of visual impairment when designing the front door of the home by offering various tactile and/or auditory indicators of a potential visitor.

Install a shelf or nook beside the apartment door, inviting residents to showcase personal items, such as holiday decorations, children's art, or sports memorabilia, which can foster direct and indirect conversations between neighbors. This small detail can enrich the greater community by transforming conventionally nondescript corridors into warm and interesting landscapes.

Offset apartment doors so residents aren't looking directly into their neighbor's unit across the hall.

Apartment doors set at an angle break up the monotony and ominousness of a long corridor.

personalized entrances

21

306
306

21

resonant **art**

As the **ultimate expression of dignity and value, art honors the human spirit** by communicating, "You deserve this experience of beauty and wonder simply because."

considerations

Select artwork that is intentional, accessible, relevant, and responsive—not imposed or colonized.

Avoid a drift toward fashion—instead, prioritize decorative elements that resonate with occupants via a historical, ecological, or cultural connection to place.

Champion an authentic narrative by curating artwork created by residents themselves or artists from the neighborhood, photographs of area landmarks or local figures, and natural imagery that reflects or connects to the surroundings.

Provide areas for displaying artwork in common spaces, such as shelves, stationary frames and clips, inviting residents to share and encouraging a sense of ownership.

Promote creativity, expression, and choice through dedicated art spaces and wood shops. A simple crafting corner equipped with coloring supplies, yarn, or wrapping paper, encourages residents to gather, experiment, and engage with self and others.

Consider interactive artistic outlets, such as rock gardens or a graffiti wall where people can stamp their name or pen a message of encouragement to others.

Invite residents to participate in the curation of artwork for their building by voting on a muralist, for example, or suggesting themes for a play structure.

22

22

Avenida del Sol

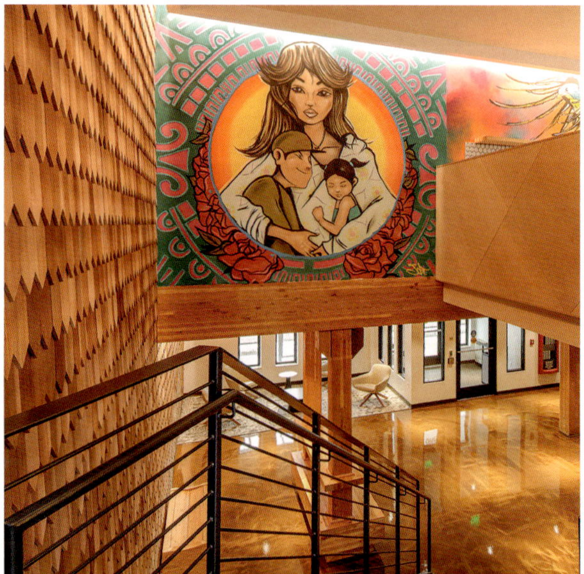

22

22

annotated **plans**

laurel **house**
supportive housing in Grand Junction, CO, for formerly unhoused youth

st.valentine's **apartments**
supportive housing in Loveland, CO

thrive
multifamily affordable housing in Denver, CO

Dignified Design cannot be reduced to a single space or to any one element within the space. Rather, it's a matter of how the three organizing principles of Dignified Design (Sensory Engagement, Nested Layers, and Identity Anchors) and their respective elements are applied in concert with one another. Further, as noted throughout this book, the 22 Elements must be employed with attention to balance and to the overall context.

Our research suggests that residents and staff experience a stronger sense of Safety, Comfort, Community, and Control as well as greater positive health and well-being outcomes when an environment incorporates a wide range of Dignified Design concepts in a holistic, artful, and responsive way.

The diagrams featured in this section illustrate the synthesis of elements at work in spaces employing a Dignified Design approach.

laurel **house**

grand junction, colorado

Completed in 2020, **Laurel House is a dynamic supportive housing development (0–30% AMI)** nestled in the sandstone canyons of Grand Junction, Colorado, offering 34 apartments for youth exiting homelessness.

Every aspect of this building's design sought to complement the organization's (Karis, Inc.) deep commitment to trauma-informed service delivery. The building is an architectural response to the client's vision of a safe and secure environment where youth can tap into curiosity, exploration, aspiration, and joy. From site plan to interior detailing, these values served as the foundation for decision-making and prioritization.

For the design team, it was important to create a warm, inviting, and approachable entry to the building. This was done by focusing on the proportions of the entrance and ensuring it was human scaled—with a playful and aspirational tree house feature at the front entrance that further steps down to a single-windowed doorway mimicking the classic front door of a house. The open lobby and community kitchen are a celebration of natural materials and warm colors, mosaic windows and daylight, nooks and nested layers, and clear sightlines with opportunities to choose your own adventure through a range of seating options and pathways throughout the space. Walking into Laurel House, residents and guests are greeted by a sign that states, "Welcome home—where memories are made, tears are shed, love is felt, and refuge is found—you belong here." This served as a guiding intention for the design and the development team who wanted the residents to feel at home, engaged and empowered, and connected to other residents and staff—in a building designed for healing, hope, and joy.

Karis, Inc., BlueLine Development, Shopworks Architecture, FCI Construction, and Flow Design Collaborative

varied **outdoor environments**
The front yards and backyards offer an array of outlets for connection, respite, and movement—including a basketball court, climbing boulder, swings and hammocks, a grill, gardens, and plenty of seating.

hearth-like **places**
In the great room, both the fireplace and the live-edge kitchen bar provide hearth-like arrangements where people can gather for conversation or share a meal.

charismatic **places**
Inspiring awe, wonder, and delight—the great room includes an array of windows, geometric pendant lights, circular nooks, playful furniture, and a sprawling mural.

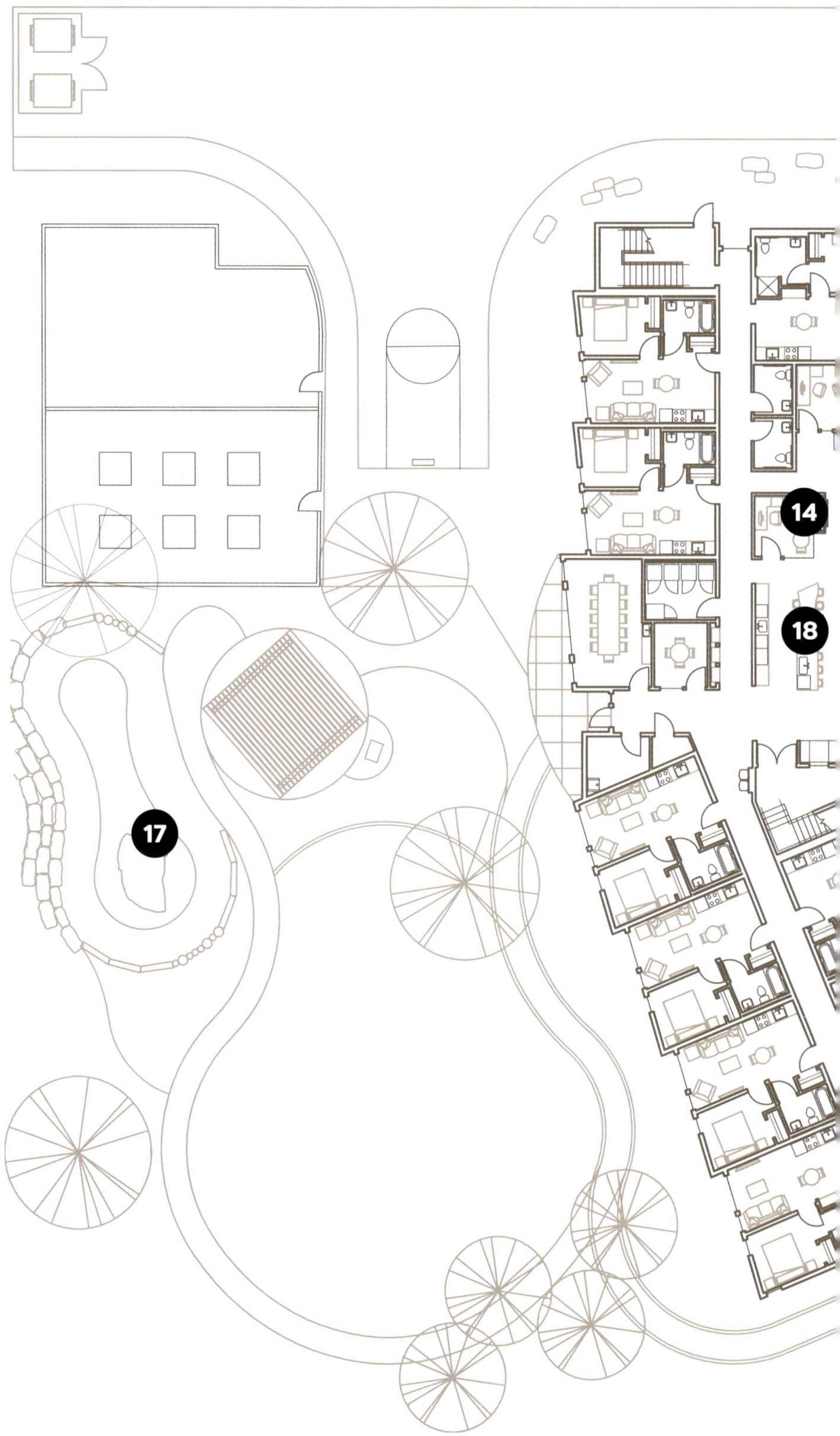

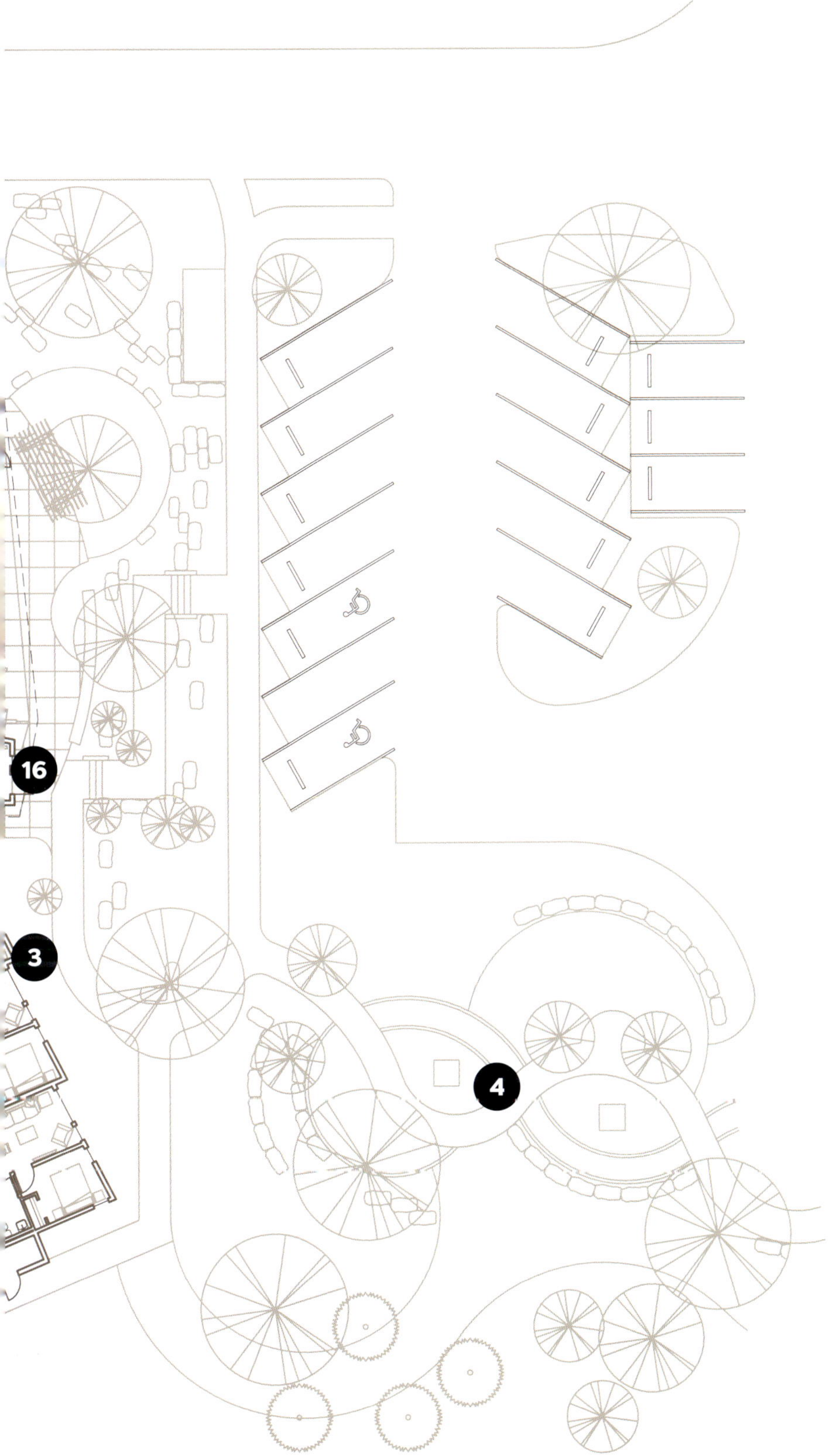

thoughtful **proportions**
The entrance of the building is segmented to suggest intimacy—from the wood cladding filled with playful windows to the modern tree house structure to the protected single, home-like door.

intentional **colors**
The colors of the building (hues of yellow and pink) mimic the sun setting on the region's rich sandstone.

living **systems**
The double helix pathway leading up to the entrance is lined with a variety of native plants to create a multisensory experience.

st. valentine's **apartments**

loveland, colorado

In 2019, the City of Loveland partnered with the University of Denver to conduct a comprehensive homelessness needs assessment, which underlined a **deep need for supportive housing in the community**.

Intent on tackling the issue head-on, Catholic Charities Housing worked tirelessly to secure local and state support in financing, land use, service provision, and neighborhood buy-in. These efforts succeeded in 2023 with the completion of Loveland's first supportive housing development, St. Valentine's Apartments, which includes 54 one- and two-bedroom units. The project demonstrates a clear commitment to meaningfully serve the community's most vulnerable unhoused neighbors, including seniors, families with young children, and individuals with disabilities.

Residents and guests are invited into the space through a protected and approachable entrance, upon which they are greeted by a friendly face at the front desk and a clear view of choices on where to move and how to engage with the space. The lobby and surrounding amenity area offer several distinct spaces, including the option to casually gather in the community kitchen, to enjoy a moment of respite and introspection on the soft seating surrounding the fireplace, or to participate in a more intimate conversation in the booths along the edge of the room. A large classroom, therapeutic meeting rooms, an enclosed courtyard, a dog run, and an open walking path outside the building offer additional spaces to formally and informally connect with self and others. The creation of St. Valentine's Apartments not only provides 54 long-term, safe homes for those who did not have an affordable place to live, but also, on a much grander scale, represents the community's deep care and commitment to meeting the needs of their neighbors with a dignified response.

Catholic Charities Housing, BlueLine Development, Shopworks Architecture, Kirsche Construction, Inc., and Flow Design Collaborative

CATHOLIC
CHARITIES
HOUSING
St. Valentine Apartments
915 E. 10th

dedicated **staff places**
A staff break room is accessible from behind the front desk, providing a layer of protection from ongoing activity while also promoting easy connection in the event of urgent need.

accessible **front desk**
The front desk is designed to be safe, clear, and welcoming with good sightlines, warm lighting, and anchoring imagery.

clear **sightlines**
The first-floor amenity space offers clear sightlines from the front desk to various seating areas, the mail area, community kitchen, enclosed courtyard, and staff offices.

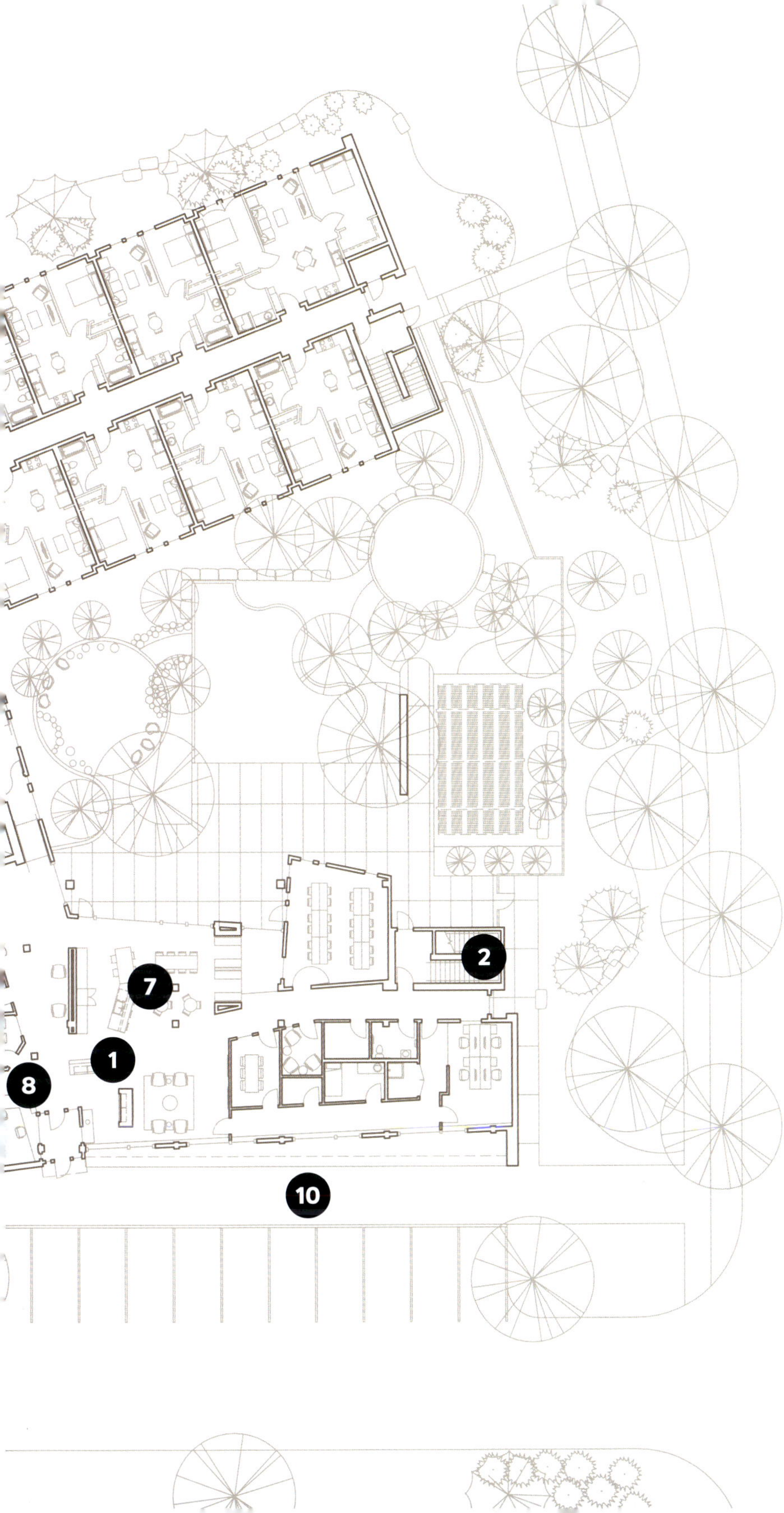

noise modulation
Glulam beams, wooden bench enclosures, and large, felt light fixtures above the community kitchen work to effectively modulate noise in the open common area.

approachable entryway
The scale of the entrance is modest and inviting with a prominent porte-cochère that maps out a path to the front door and provides cover from the elements.

enriched lighting
Large windows throughout the building welcome daylight into the entire space, illuminating areas that can feel foreboding and unpleasant.

thrive

denver, colorado

Denver Housing Authority's (DHA) Thrive is a mixed-income community comprised of 135 apartments located in the historic Sun Valley neighborhood of Denver, Colorado.

Opened in 2023, the seven-story development includes one-, two-, three-, four-, and five-bedroom units and ranges in AMI from 0–30% to market rate. By integrating a range of units across AMI levels, Thrive seeks to support a diversity of households who will represent the future of the community.

Through a five-year engagement effort, DHA worked with the local community—including residents, nonprofits, neighborhood associations, and community groups—to transform Sun Valley (0.64 square miles) from a public housing development characterized by concentrated poverty and isolation to a vibrant neighborhood with new housing, parks, commercial offerings, food markets, and residential services.

In addition to the efforts led by DHA, Shopworks performed post-occupancy research at nearby properties to hear from residents about their challenges and barriers as well as their hopes and desires related to housing. Ongoing outreach and engagement efforts informed the distinctive look and feel of Thrive throughout the design and construction process, resulting in an expansive community kitchen and indoor gathering space, multiple pathways to move throughout the building, and units organized into neighborhood clusters for a greater sense of intimacy and connection. The most prominent demonstration of these efforts is the lovable fox play structure that serves as an identity anchor for the community. As the outdoor terrace was being planned, neighborhood children were enlisted to select the playful motif that now watches over the neighborhood.

Denver Housing Authority, Shopworks Architecture, Pinkard Construction, Flow Design Collaborative, and Earthscape

attention to **neglected spaces**
The stairwells and mail area were designed with clear sightlines, daylight, views of the outdoors, plenty of space, and multiple pathways fostering safety and opportunities for social interaction.

natural **materials**
Inside the community room, beehive wooden platforms of varying heights and organic patterns offer an array of elements for sitting, playing, and curling up into.

clear **sightlines**
There are clear lines of sight across the length of the outdoor terrace as well as onto the deck from the corridors, stairwells, and apartments above.

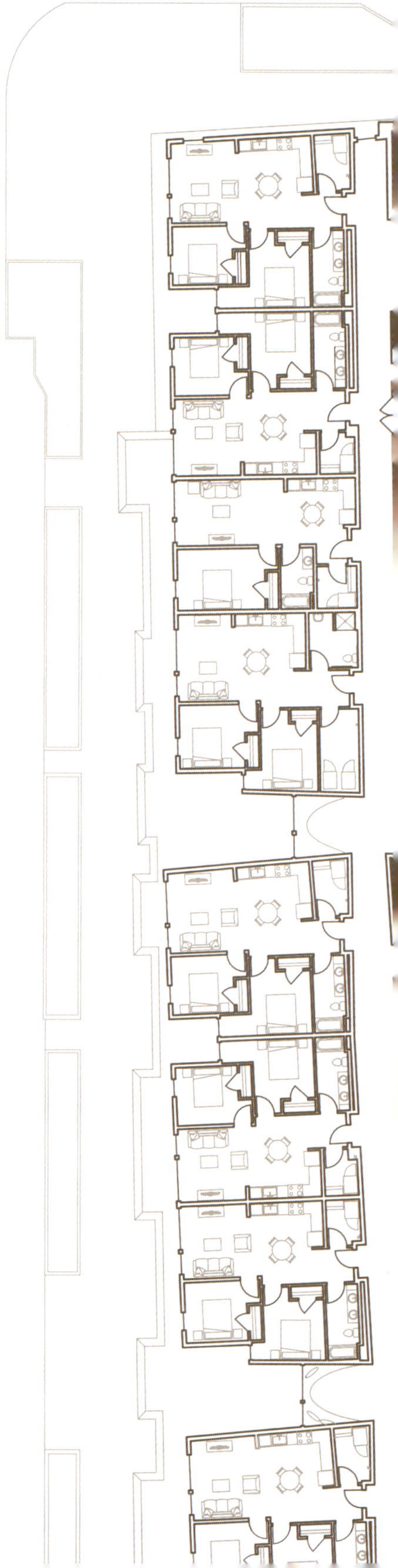

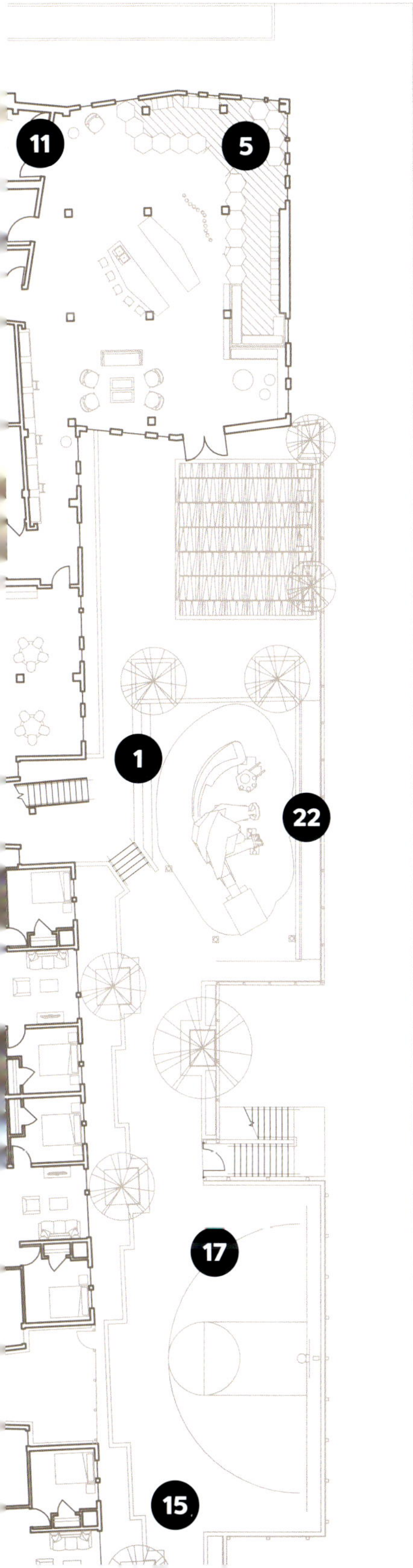

resonant **art**
Chosen by the youth, the fox play structure peers off the second-floor terrace over a neighboring schoolyard, establishing an identity anchor for the community in and around the building.

varied outdoor **environments**
The outdoor area is broken into sections for various uses, abilities, and preferences —including zones of activation, sensory engagement, respite, and social connection —all with visual access to one another.

multiple **pathways**
The terrace provides multiple access points via two centrally located exterior stairwells as well as entry/exit to the adjacent indoor community room and side doors from the corridor.

conclusion

Dignified Design does not offer a one-size-fits-all solution. The 22 Elements presented here cannot and should not function as a checklist. Rather, they are intended to promote a more holistic approach to the site plan, program, and interior design of housing once the context and lived experience of staff and residents have been deeply explored.

Dignified Design is not simply about design outcomes—in equal measure, Dignified Design is about the transformative process of thoughtfully weighing and incorporating best practice and context-specific inputs. This entails deeply understanding stress and trauma and their lasting impact on the brain and body. It involves aligning a team around a common vision, engaging, listening to, and believing end users, and incorporating all of this into the design through an iterative process. **It is the responsibility of designers to deeply explore the relationship between health and our built environment to create places that foster healing and nurture the potential of individuals and communities**.

In this same vein, healing and dignity cannot be delivered by good design alone. It requires a holistic response attending to mind, body, and spirit—supportive services and property management dedicated to a trauma-responsive approach and other best practices in housing and service delivery. Further, it requires a broader community of support, one that also biases the health and healing of people, families, communities, and all living things. Dignified Design has the potential to play a significant role in a much larger network of well-being and care.

It is our sincere hope that the 22 Elements and suggested considerations in this book promote a deeper attention to design practice and process. We look forward to continuing this discussion toward an ever-growing understanding of how to design for dignity, healing, and joy.

featured **projects**

ARROYO VILLAGE
DENVER, CO

Development/Ownership Team: Rocky Mountain Communities, The Delores Project, and BlueLine Development, Inc. | Architect: Shopworks Architecture | Contractor: I-Kota, LLC | 60-bed homeless shelter as well as 35-unit supportive housing (0-30% AMI) and 95-unit affordable housing (30-80% AMI) including one-, two-, and three-bedroom apartments.

AVENIDA DEL SOL
DENVER, CO

Developer/Owner: Gorman & Company | Architect: Shopworks Architecture | Contractor: Deneuve Construction | 90-unit affordable housing (0-80% AMI) including one, two, and three-bedroom apartments.

BLUEBIRD
BOULDER, CO

Developer/Owner: Element Properties | Architect: Shopworks Architecture | Contractor: I-Kota, LLC | 40-unit permanent supportive housing (0-30% AMI) including studio and one-bedroom apartments.

BRANDON COURTYARD
DENVER, CO

Development/Ownership Team: Volunteers of America National Services and Volunteers of America Colorado | Architect: Shopworks Architecture | Contractor: B.C. Builders LLC | 104-unit affordable housing (0-80% AMI) including one-, two-, and three-bedroom apartments. The project caters to veterans.

BRUSH VILLAGE II
BRUSH, CO

Developer/Owner: Northpointe Development Corporation | Architect: Shopworks Architecture | Contractor: Krische Construction, Inc. | 45-unit affordable housing (30-60% AMI) including one- and two-bedroom apartments.

CADENCE
FORT COLLINS, CO

Developer/Owner: Volunteers of America National Services | Architect: Shopworks Architecture | Contractor: B.C. Builders LLC | 55-unit senior affordable housing (20-80% AMI) including one- and two-bedroom apartments.

CHANDA CENTER FOR HEALTH
LAKEWOOD, CO

Developer/Owner: Chanda Center for Health | Architect: Shopworks Architecture | Contractor: Hensel Phelps | Healthcare environment supporting people with physical disabilities to receive integrated therapy.

CHARITY'S HOUSE
DENVER, CO

Development/Ownership Team: Community Outreach Service Center and BlueLine Development, Inc. | Architect: Shopworks Architecture | Contractor: Deneuve Construction | 36–unit supportive housing (0-30% AMI) includes one-bedroom apartments.

THE ELISABETTA
DENVER, CO

Development/Ownership Team: Laradon and Gorman & Company | Architect: Shopworks Architecture | Contractor: Deneuve Construction | 91-unit affordable housing (0-80% AMI) includes one-, two-, three-, and four-bedroom apartments. The project is working in partnership with the Laradon School to operate an adult day program on the ground floor.

ESPERO
DURANGO, CO

Development/Ownership Team: Housing Solutions for the Southwest and BlueLine Development, Inc. | Architect: Shopworks Architecture | Contractor: FCI Constructors | 40-unit supportive housing (0-30% AMI) includes one-bedroom apartments. The project is the first supportive housing in Durango.

FOUNDRY APARTMENTS
ENGLEWOOD, CO

Developer/Owner: Southwest Development, LLC | Architect: Shopworks Architecture | Contractor: Catamount Constructors, Inc. | 70-unit affordable housing (0-60% AMI) includes one- and two-bedroom apartments.

HIGHLAND JUNCTION
DENVER, CO

Developer/Owner: Zakhem Real Estate Group | Architect: Shopworks Architecture | Contractor: I-Kota, LLC | 39-unit market-rate housing includes studios, one-, and two-bedroom apartments.

featured **projects**

INDY STREET FLATS
LAKEWOOD, CO

Developer/Owner: Metro West Housing Solutions | Architect: Shopworks Architecture | Contractor: Taylor Kohrs | 115-unit affordable housing (0-60% AMI) includes one-, two-, and three-bedroom apartments. The development includes the renovation of an on-site Masonic temple into micro-units as well as rehabilitation of existing walk-up units.

THE IVES
WHEAT RIDGE, CO

Developer/Owner: Foothills Regional Housing | Architect: Shopworks Architecture | Contractor: Calcon Constructors, Inc. | 50-unit affordable housing (0-60% AMI) including one-bedroom apartments.

LA VIÑA APARTMENTS
DENVER, CO

Developer/Owner: Columbia Ventures, LLC | Architect: Shopworks Architecture | Contractor: I-Kota, LLC | 150-unit affordable housing (0-80% AMI) including one-, two-, and three-bedroom apartments. The ground floor includes a healthcare clinic and retail space.

LAUREL HOUSE
GRAND JUNCTION, CO

Development/Ownership Team: Karis, Inc and BlueLine Development, Inc. | Architect: Shopworks Architecture | Contractor: FCI Constructors | 34-unit supportive housing (0-30% AMI) designated for youth (18–24 years old) including one-bedroom apartments.

MASON PLACE
FORT COLLINS, CO

Developer/Owner: Housing Catalyst | Architect: Shopworks Architecture | Contractor: I-Kota, LLC | 60-unit supportive housing (0-30% AMI) including one- and two-bedroom apartments. The project is an adaptive reuse of a former movie theater.

MI CASA RESOURCE CENTER
DENVER, CO

Development/Ownership Team: Gorman & Company and Mi Casa Resource Center | Architect: Shopworks Architecture | Contractor: Deneuve Construction | 20,000 SF office space serving the Mi Casa Resource Center, a nonprofit providing resources to advance the economic prosperity of the Latino community. Offices are located on the ground floor of the Terraza del Sol Apartments.

MIREMONTE
DURANGO, CO

Developer/Owner: Volunteers of America National Services | Architect: Shopworks Architecture | Contractor: FCI Constructors | 53-unit senior affordable housing (0-60% AMI) including one- and two-bedroom apartments.

THE MOTHERSHIP
DENVER, CO

Development/Ownership Team: Urban Peak and BlueLine Development, Inc. | Architect: Shopworks Architecture | Contractor: Deneuve Construction | Congregate shelter and neighborhood-style transitional housing serving more than 130 youth experiencing homelessness.

OAK 140
FORT COLLINS, CO

Developer/Owner: Housing Catalyst | Architect: Shopworks Architecture | Contractor: Calcon Constructors, Inc. | 79-unit affordable housing (30-80% AMI) including one- and two-bedroom apartments.

OVERLOOK AT POWERS PARK
LITTLETON, CO

Developer/Owner: South Metro Housing Options | Architect: Shopworks Architecture | Contractor: Calcon Constructors, Inc. | 51-unit senior affordable housing (30-60% AMI) including one-bedroom apartments.

PROVIDENCE AT THE-HEIGHTS
AURORA, CO

Development/Ownership Team: Second Chance Center, Inc. and BlueLine Development, Inc. | Architect: Shopworks Architecture | Contractor: Calcon Constructors, Inc. | 50-unit supportive housing (0-30% AMI) including one- and two-bedroom apartments. The project caters to individuals who have exited incarceration.

RHONDA'S PLACE
DENVER, CO

Development/Ownership Team: REDI Corporation and BlueLine Development, Inc. | Architect: Shopworks Architecture | Contractor: Calcon Constructors, Inc. | 49-unit supportive housing (0-30% AMI) including one-bedroom apartments.

featured **projects**

THE STELLA
DENVER, CO

Development/Ownership Team: Gorman & Company, Inc. and Laradon | Architect: Shopworks Architecture | Contractor: Deneuve Construction | 132-unit affordable housing (30-80% AMI) including two-, three-, and four-bedroom apartments. The ground floor space is operated by the Laradon School.

ST. VALENTINE'S APARTMENTS
LOVELAND, CO

Development/Ownership Team: Catholic Charities Housing and BlueLine Development, Inc. | Architect: Shopworks Architecture | Contractor: KCI Construction | 54-unit supportive housing (0-30% AMI) including one- and two-bedroom apartments. The project is the first supportive housing development in Loveland.

TAWI KAAN
CORTEZ, CO

Development/Ownership Team: BlueLine Development, Inc. and The Piñon Project | Architect: Shopworks Architecture | Contractor: FCI Constructors | 42-unit supportive housing (0-30% AMI) including one-, two- and three-bedroom apartments. Project was created in partnership with the Ute Mountain Ute Tribe.

TERRAZA DEL SOL
DENVER, CO

Development/Ownership Team: Gorman & Company, Inc., Terraza del Sol, LLC, and Mi Casa Resource Center | Architect: Shopworks Architecture | Contractor: Deneuve Construction | 42-unit affordable housing (30-60% AMI) including one-, two-, and three-bedroom apartments.

THRIVE
DENVER, CO

Developer/Owner: Denver Housing Authority | Architect: Shopworks Architecture | Contractor: Pinkard Construction Company | 135-unit mixed-income housing (30-100% AMI) including one-, three-, four-, and five-bedroom apartments serving families in the Sun Valley neighborhood.

TREMONT TOWNHOMES
DENVER, CO

Developer/Owner: Brad O'Neil | Architect: Shopworks Architecture | Contractor: I-Kota, LLC | 24-unit mixed-income housing (20-100% AMI) including one-, two-, and three-bedroom townhomes.

VALOR ON THE FAX
DENVER, CO

Development/Ownership Team: Brothers Redevelopment, Inc. and the Brain Injury Alliance of Colorado | Architect: Shopworks Architecture | Contractor: Calcon Constructors, Inc. | 72-unit supportive housing (0-30% AMI) including one-, two-, and three-bedroom apartments. The project is the first supportive housing in the country designed specifically for residents with brain injuries.

WARREN RESIDENCES
DENVER, CO

Development/Ownership Team: Saint Francis Center and BlueLine Development, Inc. | Architect: Shopworks Architecture | Contractor: Taylor Kohrs | 48-unit supportive housing (0-30% AMI) including studio-style apartments and congregate living space. The project is a renovation of a historic United Methodist Church.

ZINNIA APARTMENTS
LONGMONT, CO

Developer/Owner: Element Properties | Architect: Shopworks Architecture | Contractor: I-Kota, LLC | 55-unit supportive housing (0-30% AMI) including one-bedroom apartments.

photo **captions**

front cover, Mothership | front exterior

2, Tawi Kaan | community room

5, (clockwise from top left): Arroyo Village | front exterior; Rhonda's Place | courtyard; Cadence | patio, Rhonda's Place | stairwell; The Elisabetta | laundry room; Oak 140 | community room

6, Chanda Center for Health | entrance

7, St. Valentine's Apartments | community kitchen light fixture detail (left); Bluebird | community room (center); Warren Residences | apartment entrances (right)

8–9, St. Valentine's Apartments | community kitchen light fixture detail

10, Mason Place | atrium

12–13, Thrive | stairwell

14–15, Avenida del Sol | community kitchen and mail area

16–17, Thrive | terrace

18, Providence at the Heights | corridor along staff offices

20, Bluebird | community room

21, Espero | stairwell

22–23, St. Valentine's Apartments | community room and kitchen

24, (clockwise from top left): La Viña Apartments | lit entrance to courtyard; Mothership | seating area in cafeteria; Espero | stairwell; Bluebird | lobby; Arroyo Village | exterior detail

26, Oak 140 | exterior sketch

27, Oak 140 | terrace

28–29, Valor on the Fax | exterior

30, Rhonda's Place | exterior landscaping detail

32, Mason Place | atrium plant detail

33, Brandon Courtyard | community room plant detail (top); Oak 140 | lobby (bottom)

34–35, La Viña Apartments | courtyard mural by Bimmer Torres

36, The Stella | lobby

38–39, Bluebird | front exterior

40–41, Warren Residences | community room and kitchen

43, Highland Junction | courtyard

44–45, Brandon Courtyard | community room and kitchen

47, Valor on the Fax | terrace fountain detail

48–49, Oak 140 | lobby

50, Overlook at Powers Park | community room

51, St. Valentine's Apartments | community kitchen

52–53, La Viña Apartments | lobby

54–55, Bluebird | community room

56, Mason Place | front desk and mail area

58, Providence at the Heights | front desk

59, St. Valentine's Apartments | front desk

60, Mothership | neighborhood kitchen

62–63, La Viña Apartments | front exterior

64–65, Rhonda's Place | exterior with sketch of first-floor height detail

66, Thrive | front entrance

68, St. Valentine's Apartments | exterior sketch

69, Laurel House | pathway to front entrance

70, Foundry Apartments | entrance

71, Mi Casa Resource Center | entrance and mural by Carlos Frésquez

72, **74–75**, Rhonda's Place | laundry room

76, The Ives | public restroom (left); Avenida del Sol | mail area (right)

77, The Elisabetta | bike room

78–79, La Viña Apartments | lobby mailbox detail

80, Miremonte | staff office

82–83, Mi Casa Resource Center | staff offices and break area

84–85, Indy Street Flats | staff offices

86, Mi Casa Resource Center | floor plan sketch

88, The Ives | community room seating

89, The Ives | community room seating (left); The Ives | children's area outside offices (top right); The Ives | laundry room seating (bottom right)

90–91, Laurel House | community room

92, Tawi Kaan | courtyard sketch

93, Oak 140 | community room fireplace detail

94–95, Providence at the Heights | lobby

96–97, Tawi Kaan | community room and kitchen

98–99, Rhonda's Place | lobby and community kitchen

101, Mason Place | atrium

102–103, The Stella | staff offices

104–105, Thrive | lobby and surrounding staff offices

106, Laurel House | front entrance

107, Henninger Legacy Homes | exterior elevation sketch

108–109, Laurel House | community room and window detail

110–111, Mothership | exterior

112–113, Warren Residences | corridor and community room balcony

114, Laurel House | rear exterior

116–117, La Viña Apartments | courtyard

118, The Howick | courtyard sketch

119, Valor on the Fax | terrace

120–121, Thrive | terrace and city view

122–123, Warren Residences | apartment entrances

photo **captions**

125, (clockwise from top left): The Ives | lobby wall detail; Oak 140 | community room fireplace detail; Brandon Courtyard | lobby screen detail; The Stella | lobby wall detail; The Elisabetta | elevator screen detail; Indy Street Flats | community room wall detail

126, Brush Village II | community room and wall nook detail

127, La Viña Apartments | community room television landing

128, Indy Street Flats | community room and kitchen

129, Indy Street Flats | public bathroom

131, Laurel House | front pathway to fountain

132–133, Thrive | hallway

134, Avenida del Sol | corridor

135, Zinnia Apartments | corridors

137–139, Zinnia Apartments | furnished apartment

141, Tremont Townhomes | exterior

142, The Elisabetta | artwork by youth used to create custom apartment number plaques

143, The Elisabetta | apartment entrance with personalized nook and custom apartment number plaque

144, Charity's House | exterior mural by Thomas Evans a.k.a. Detour

146–147, The Stella | community room mural by Jeremy Silas Ulibarri a.k.a. Jolt

148, (clockwise from top left): Mi Casa Resource Center | conference room mural by Carlos Frésquez; Avenida del Sol | exterior mural by Thomas Evans a.k.a. Detour; Overlook at Powers Park | community room mural by Jason T. Graves; The Stella | lobby mural by Jeremy Silas Ulibarri a.k.a. Jolt; Overlook at Powers Park | exterior mural by Jason T. Graves; La Viña Apartments | exterior lighting

149, Thrive | terrace play structure by Earthscape

150–151, Mi Casa Resource Center | exterior mural by Ratha Sok and Bimmer Torres

152–153, Thrive | lobby

167, Thrive | terrace play structure

back cover, Oak 140 | lobby

Avenida del Sol
5048

EXIT
148